*Flir*tology

*Flir*tology

Stop swiping,
start talking
and find love.

Jean Smith

BANTAM PRESS

LONDON · NEW YORK · TORONTO · SYDNEY · AUCKLAND

TRANSWORLD PUBLISHERS
61–63 Uxbridge Road, London W5 5SA
www.penguin.co.uk

Transworld is part of the Penguin Random House group of companies
whose addresses can be found at global.penguinrandomhouse.com

First published in Great Britain in 2018 by Bantam Press
an imprint of Transworld Publishers

A CIP catalogue record for this book
is available from the British Library.

ISBN 9780593079416

Typeset in 11/16 pt Minion by Jouve (UK), Milton Keynes
Printed and bound in Great Britain by Clays Ltd, Bungay, Suffolk

Penguin Random House is committed to a sustainable
future for our business, our readers and our planet. This book
is made from Forest Stewardship Council® certified paper.

1 3 5 7 9 10 8 6 4 2

This book is dedicated to you and me and our pact: be curious, be open-minded, and be questioning. I will, if you will.

Contents

Acknowledgements

There are many people I'd like to thank for helping to make this book happen: to Celia Hayley, who helped pull it together; amongst the cakes and cups of tea, you made this process fun and effortless. Watching your elegant brain work, in structuring mode in particular, is a rare treat. I wish all collaborations could be this sweet. My literary agent, Rob Dinsdale, for having the foresight to see that the world was ready for Flirtology and for connecting me with the right people to help spread the word. My publisher extraordinaire, Michelle Signore, and the amazing team at Transworld, who are the perfect fits for Flirtology. And I'm hugely grateful to Alexandra, Alexander and Jake at Conville and Walsh. To my creative genius friends: Amanda, Simon, Todd. Thank you for your time, humour and invaluable feedback.

To all the people over the years who have come on my flirting tours, who came to me for coaching, allowed me to interview them for my flirting research and attended my lectures. I have changed names and the details of your stories throughout, but I know there would be no book without you. Actually, there would be no Flirtology without you. We are all teachers, and we are all learners. Thank you for being both for me.

To my husband Nic. Everything is possible with your unyielding support and boundless talent. (Besides, you're a blast!)

Introduction

IT'S FRIDAY NIGHT. Jane has put on her favourite outfit and is feeling hopeful. She feels that she has been single for too long and is ready to do something about it. She has made a resolution to force herself to go out every weekend. Tonight, her friend is having a party and there must be somebody interesting there, surely.

An hour into the party, she sees someone attractive over by the drinks table. She wants to talk to him, but she can't see herself just interrupting the conversation he's having. When she finally works up the nerve, he is gone. In the kitchen, she exchanges a smile with someone else and wishes she could think of something to say, but that moment is gone too, and now so is he. Midnight rolls around and, other than a white-wine headache, her accomplishments are limited. She goes home, and that's when the negativity kicks in. 'I am doing everything I can. I go out. I try. It's impossible to meet people!' That is the moment that she decides to be even more proactive. That very night, she signs up to an online dating website, because now she is *really* serious about meeting someone; no more messing around.

Saturday passes in a blur. All of Jane's usual weekend activities – a run, coffee at her local cafe and a leisurely read of the papers – are put aside. By the time she has created a profile and begun sorting through the masses of other people's profiles, Saturday is gone, and then so is Sunday. However, all of her efforts are not in vain. She has begun messaging a few potential prospects and is having fun. Most of the week is spent sending and returning messages. A few people quickly drop off the radar. However, she has managed to arrange a drink for Friday night with one of them. Yes!

Second attempt. It's Friday night. Jane has put on her favourite outfit and is feeling hopeful. She has made a resolution to force herself to go out every weekend, and now it's happening, she thinks.

The person she has been flirting with all week online, the one who is funny, interesting and with whom she has so much in common, has just walked in. Her heart sinks. The only way this could be the same person from the profile picture is if it was 2008. Never mind. She has been enjoying the message exchanges, and she's here now anyway. She'll give him a chance. And then they sit down and begin talking. Jane wonders who this person is sitting in front of her. He is nothing like what he seemed online. Because she is new to this whole thing and doesn't really know how to end it, she ends up spending five hours with him, the whole time thinking of how she could make a getaway without hurting his feelings. Midnight rolls around and, other than a white-wine headache, her accomplishments are limited. Here she was hoping for the happy-ever-after to begin, and all she has is the beginnings of a hangover. She goes home, and that's when the negativity kicks in. 'I am doing everything I can. I go out. I try. It's impossible to meet people!' This is the moment Jane decides that she will be single forever . . .

Whether you are a man or a woman, if you are currently single, perhaps you can relate to this story. In my work as a Flirtologist, I use the principles of social anthropology to steer people through the thickets of social interaction. I have heard hundreds of variations on this scenario from both women and men. When it comes to meeting people, everyone is doing what they think is right, what they have been told is right, and they are baffled as to why things keep going so wrong. I can see with clarity where just one step done differently could have resulted in a more satisfactory outcome.

People come to me desperate to know how to produce results. They have been through the process multiple times. They have tried getting out there; they want to mingle, date or find partners, but they have come to realize that something isn't working. The conclusion they draw is that they are 'bad at flirting'. And then a helpful friend suggests the internet. Figuring nothing else is working, they give it a try. Because surely that will solve their problems: a vast arena where you can find people, whether you're a great flirt or not. Problem is, that isn't working either.

In the last ten years, there has been a huge upsurge in the use of online dating and dating apps. In 2007, Apple launched the first iPhone, allowing us to bring the entire digital world with us in our pockets, thereby kicking off an era of 24-hour connectivity;

since then it has become ever easier to have conversations with people via a screen. Dating apps and websites have proliferated, catering to more and more specific tastes. We are told we can find anyone – the perfect match – through the use of clever algorithms. But a funny thing has happened. As the digital revolution in dating services has gained pace, I have found people are becoming *more* hungry for guidance in how to interact meaningfully with others face to face.

There are 91 million people around the world using dating apps. This is a staggering number, and yet the evidence shows that as far as dating is concerned, the answers do not lie behind a screen. According to Pew, a leading think tank, 49,250,000 single adults in the US have tried online dating. That is nearly 50 million people! But the number of Americans in a marriage or committed relationship who met their significant other online? Only 5 per cent. And even among those who have been with their spouse or partner for five years or less – well within the era when online dating has been popular – 88 per cent met their partner offline, without the help of a dating site. In the UK, 15 million singles are registered for online dating. But a study surveying 18–35-year-olds (what you might think of as the digital generation) found that more than 80 per cent of their respondents still met their partners in real-life situations: through the 'traditional' routes of friends, social situations and work. Only 10 per cent met through online dating and 6 per cent through social media.

And it's worth remembering that the online dating industry is not a charity. Its estimated worth is more than £2 billion globally, £300 million a year in the UK alone. The dating-site business model relies on people *not* finding a match, therefore continuing to pay their subscription. Sounds a bit contradictory, doesn't it?

And, in fact, we already know all this in our hearts; in a study of Americans, only 20 per cent believe online dating is a good way to meet a romantic partner, and even fewer (15 per cent) report having significant success with it. All of which begs the question, why are the other 80 per cent still trying it?

'I'm too busy to date' seems to be a popular reason for moving online. But the average internet dater spends 13.5 hours per week on their internet profile for only 1.5 hours of actual real-life face time. This does not seem like an efficient use of time, even before you factor in how many 'real-life faces' you have to sit in front of before you find one that you like (or that matches their profile pic). And, quite likely, you might have noticed all the time-wasters. It's not your imagination. Thirty-three per cent of online daters – that's a third of them – have never actually gone on a date with someone they met through an online dating service. Looked at like that – what are we all doing out there?

Far from the digital dating phenomenon doing away with the need to approach people in the real world, it seems that people need help more than ever.

Humans are social animals, designed to form close relationships and communities. Newborn babies can fail to thrive or may even die without touch. Imprisonment is bad, solitary isolation almost unimaginable. Humans first moved around in tribes: groups of 30–50 people. As populations grew, the tribe would break off and a new one would be created, because if numbers became greater than this, it resulted in a lack of social cohesion. The numbers in which we arrange ourselves has grown – the UN predicts that by 2050 nearly 70 per cent of us will be living in cities. This does not mean, however, that our need for community has changed. But somehow we seem to be attempting to meet this need online. How have we got ourselves into the situation where we now have 500 Facebook friends, a thousand followers on Twitter, and five separate WhatsApp conversations going on at any one time, but we are still feeling cut off? Numerous studies show us that all this social-media activity can serve only to make us feel more depressed. Recent data on loneliness and reduction in close friendships seems to support the idea that the internet is not improving our social connections. To make things worse, studies have shown that our real support networks are shrinking.

The question that needs to be asked is: can the digital world really replace that need for human-to-human socialization? At first, it seems very convenient; social connection no longer needs a car, phone call or plan – just a click. It's also true that we momentarily feel better when we engage with others virtually, but research shows these connections are often superficial and ultimately dissatisfying. One study concludes that the digital world temporarily enhances the social satisfaction and behaviour of lonely people, who are more likely to go online when they feel isolated or depressed, but that this is also a major reason the internet makes us lonely: we attempt to substitute real relationships with online relationships. And, the report concludes, this is 'not an effective alternative for offline social interactions'.

As the psychologist Adam Alter explained in a recent TED talk, amidst the ever-increasing time we spend on our screens, there are some apps that make us feel good. He cites examples of reading, health, education and relaxation apps. But others actively make us feel bad. He points the finger at social media, gaming and, crucially, dating apps. And it is the ones that make us feel worse that we engage with the most: three times more in fact. We spend 27 minutes per day on each of the 'negative' apps compared to nine minutes per day on the 'positive' ones.

The smartphone is more than just a faster, pocket-sized computer; it can also be seen as a driver of social and behavioural change, causing a shift in the way we act offline as well as on. Do you remember the time – not long ago – when you could walk into a cafe and people would not all be hunched over their phones? According to a British study, we check our phones on average 221 times a day – about every 4.3 minutes. Because, with the convenience of a tiny device, we are now connected whenever and wherever.

In a 2015 Pew survey, nearly half of 18–29-year-olds questioned said they used their phones to avoid interacting with others around them. Before smartphones, we also had ways to avoid people. Burying one's head in a newspaper on a morning commute is a good example. But we couldn't whip out those newspapers while standing on the edges of a party, in the checkout queue or even walking down the street. Newspapers couldn't be used as shields at any given moment. What did we do before we had built-in protection to avoid others around us? Oh yes, we spoke to each other. And those conversations led to all sorts of things – love affairs, friendships, the chance to break down stereotypes (very easy to solidify when we aren't doing anything to combat them).

In fact, the very *presence* of technology can hinder genuine offline connection. Simply having a phone near by caused pairs of strangers to rate their conversation as less meaningful, their conversation partners as less empathetic, and their new relationship as less close than strangers with a notebook near by instead.

So, why are we choosing connectivity over connection?

There are all sorts of reasons why the screen has become so ubiquitous, but when it comes to dating, I have a specific theory. It's because the potential thrill of a real-life encounter cannot compete with an even stronger feeling: the fear of not being accepted. This feeling is so strong that even the mere thought of it happening changes our behaviour. People take to their screens because they think they can hide behind them; they believe the sting of one's online persona being rejected will hurt less than the sting of rejection in the flesh. Indeed, this was one of the founding principles of at least one major dating app – to create a space where men in particular would be shielded from the perceived slight of an outright refusal. We act in a way that we think will decrease the chances of experiencing this pain. And this is the perceived allure of the internet: a place where we can test the waters, see how people respond to us without really having to put ourselves out there, without having to experience the full brunt of not being accepted.

At first glance, the internet seems to offer a magical opportunity: the possibility of endless connections without putting our real selves on the line. But this is a mirage, and it comes at the cost of forgoing real potential successes. Besides the fact we are missing out on countless opportunities in trying to protect ourselves, the irony is that we cannot even be certain that this safeguarding is working. Could all of our safety measures be for naught? Have we trapped ourselves into an affair with our electronic devices for no good reason?

The solution? We must go back to the basics, back to good old-fashioned face-to-face interactions. But here is the modern twist. What if I told you that you can learn to do this without having to worry about the pain of rejection? This is one of the many things that I am offering you with Flirtology.

What is Flirtology?

First, what exactly is *flirting*? I travelled to the cities of New York, Paris, London and Stockholm to find out. As part of my research for my Masters dissertation, I interviewed over two hundred people and explored cafes, supermarkets, nightclubs, parties, whilst living like a local. The goal was to uncover how people in each of these cities flirted. Someone had to do it. Why not me? The result of this, and of over ten years spent working with would-be flirters, is that I don't need to guess how people flirt; I have the research with the answers. I will be sharing some of this research and the responses people gave me throughout the book.

The results were surprising. Flirting is just one little word, but it seems that the ways in which people understand it are endless. Is it about seduction or is it about fun? Do you do it to get dates or do you do it at the checkout to liven the day? Do you flirt only with people to whom you are attracted or is it an automatic response? For some people, there is a definite sexual undertone, to others it is just 'charming someone to make them feel good; it's a way of life'. And determining whom we flirt with depends again on whom we ask. Some say that flirting can be enjoyed between colleagues at work – 'it helps to get things done more quickly'. For others, it's only done with those they fancy. In other words, there are as many different types of flirting as there are people wanting to interact with each other.

If there are a million different definitions of flirting, what then is Flirtology? Well, that I can tell you with 100 per cent assurance. I should know, as I created the word over a decade ago. The base of the word, flirt-ology, means 'the study of flirting', and in essence Flirtology comprises two facets: the science of flirting and the art of interaction.

Flirtology is based on social science, the academic study of what it means to be a social being. Approaching flirting as a science means that if you feel that you are not currently good at it, do not despair. There is hope! Flirting is a learned behaviour, and a good flirt can be made. This is done by starting with some basic tools that I learned during my training in social anthropology. Anthropologic methodologies help break through created fears and negative expectations to show us what is actually true. Flirtology applies logical scientific thinking to all those things you 'just know', bringing clarity to this most subjective and emotional of areas.

But Flirtology is more than a science; it's also an art – the art of interaction. Once you have used the clarity of the scientific method to unshackle yourself from a whole load of unhelpful assumptions, you are then free to actually *enjoy* the experience of meeting people, talking to them, going on dates, connecting, finding The One. The artist Georgia O'Keeffe says that art to her is 'filling a space in a beautiful way'. This is exactly how I see Flirtology and the art of interaction: filling the space in a beautiful way. It is about having the best possible interactions with those around us. Whatever your goals are, Flirtology is here to help you delight in the quest and to have a marvellous time while doing it.

How did I come to be a Flirtologist?

As the eldest sister to two younger brothers, you could say that I was born into this role. I have fond memories of coaching my brothers and their friends on the fine art of engaging with women. One particular memory is of visiting one of my brothers at college and him dragging a reluctant friend over to me with the encouraging instruction to, 'Ask my sister; she's really good at this stuff.' It didn't take much more convincing for the outpouring of woe and confusion to begin.

My fascination with how people live their lives took me to a degree in Cultural Anthropology at Kansas University. After I left, I began exploring the world. You could say that I haven't stopped. My stint at Kansas University was the last time that I lived in the United States. Since then I have travelled to over sixty countries and have lived in six. People-watching in so many different places was fascinating: it was like my degree subject come to life. My interest in anthropology has always been drawn to the contemporary and my immediate surroundings. How do we exist and prosper as a social species today, in our modern world?

I have now lived in my beloved London for the last 18 years. And that brings us to how Flirtology really got going. Upon first moving to London in 2000, I looked around and thought, 'Why is no one speaking with each other?' In a culture that thrives on understatement, the trick of British flirting is to not actually appear as if you are flirting. It's showing you are interested, but in a way that no one can understand. I therefore spent much of the first years of my life in London missing signals – until I learned the unwritten rules of British culture. I identified that the only time to speak to someone that you don't know is Thursday– Saturday night, after 8 p.m. and after at least three drinks. *Now* I know that these unwritten rules of behaviour mostly revolve around how the Brits think one should act towards others: polite and courteous while maintaining a certain distance. These are very nice ways to behave in a civilized society. But they are cer- tainly not useful for people wanting to connect with each other. And as I have since discovered, the reserved Brits, like everyone else, are also craving more interaction with each other.

So, I created the Fearless Flirting Tours of London, interactive tours where I teach people how to approach and talk to strangers. Being on the forefront of the flirting world in this way also fired my curiosity even more: was there a more rigorous way I could analyse and use the knowledge I was acquiring? This led to my Master's degree in Social Anthropology at SOAS, University of London. I was interested specifically in flirting cultures – how do we flirt in our modern-day society? And thus, Flirtology was born: a company to help people apply the traditional science of anthropology to the world of flirtation and romantic connections. When I began my flirting tours 12 years ago, people thought it was a 'cool idea', but most didn't feel they *needed* me. Now, I have private clients and corporate clients, run flirting tours and digital courses, hold seminars and workshops, all fuelled by people's need to make connections. I am inundated with people trying to get a handle on how to interact with others. This book is a distillation of the wisdom I have gleaned from all of these encounters over the years. (Though for the purposes of sharing this with you I have made changes to the details of people's stories to protect their privacy.)

What can Flirtology do for you?

Contained within this book is a fun, efficient, streamlined and scientifically researched approach to the important skill of flirting. How are we going to find love if we are hesitant even about simple interactions? I want to show everyone – women and men – the best ways to get out there into the real world and find love.

Calling on the experience I've assimilated over more than ten years of steering clients through the thickets of the flirting world, and through extensive anthropological research undertaken in four different countries, the book will:

- debunk the myths that surround flirting
- give you sure-fire ways to avoid those awkward tongue-tied moments

- make sure you never fear rejection again
- make you believe that you too are a fabulous flirt
- help you pinpoint what it is you are looking for
- unlock the secrets of my H.O.T. A.P.E. system to bring out your inner flirt
- encourage you to practise, practise and practise (and have fun while doing it)
- give you the confidence to speak to anyone, anywhere
- get results, without ever compromising who you are.

Who is Flirtology for?

The book is intended for both women and men. I find it strange when 'experts' address one particular gender with advice, as if we are different species. Women and men are more similar than different. And, mostly, we have the same concerns, problems and issues. Sometimes people seem to think that all this relationship, touchy-feely stuff should be left to the womenfolk. Which is why if you are a woman talking about these subjects and reading this book, no one bats an eye. But the societal expectation for men is that they are either born players, meant to know everything already, or that they should stick to what they know best: talking about sports and mowing the lawn. But, actually, I find that men are just as curious and just as keen to learn about Flirtology as women. Up until a few years ago, a sighting of a male participant on my Fearless Flirting tours was rare. Most preferred to learn digitally via my online Flirtology courses, happy to brush up on the magical ways of women from the safety of their living rooms. However, that has changed.

Currently, most of my flirting tours are made up of half men and half women. And all of my private clients are men. This is part of a big shift I have seen in recent years. I see this influx of men happy to come forward and ask for help as a renaissance, and I like it.

So, this book is for everyone who wants to improve their flirting life. It will answer the million-dollar questions – ones I've been asked hundreds of times by people anxious for my help:

- 'Why can I flirt with someone whom I don't find attractive but can't with those whom I do?'
- 'How can I tell if someone is flirting with me?'
- 'How can I be a more confident flirt?'
- 'How can I ask someone out without feeling awkward?'

And by the end of it you will have the answers to all of these questions and feel confident in approaching anyone you want.

The good news is that all the tools for successful flirting are right at your fingertips already. You can start immediately; there's no need to go to special venues or learn a lot of complicated tips. Flirtology is not about games, it's not about rules and it's not about tricks. It's a way of presenting your most confident and authentic self so that you attract the people you want to attract. It's about increasing and improving *all* our human interactions, not just putting on a pouty face when we see someone attractive. It's about helping others to feel good themselves and then getting it back tenfold, not about trying to get other people to make us feel good. It's about realizing that flirting is not just a means to an end; you don't only flirt if you want something. And it's about being efficient.

Finding a partner shouldn't be an extra burden on top of your already busy life. It can be something that happens while you are out and about, having an interesting and fulfilling existence.

In my private coaching, I do not try to help clients go on *more* dates; I want them to have better-quality ones with the right people. Success is not gauged by picking up the most phone numbers at a party; it is about feeling comfortable in approaching and talking to as many people as you can while you're there. It's not about more swipes on Tinder; it's about the real world and meeting people who are reacting to your own, three-dimensional, fabulous self.

Flirtology is about enhancing every aspect of your life. It asks us to meet the world with an open, curious mind, to enjoy and improve every interaction that we have, ranging from our close friendships to the receptionist at work. It asks us to thread its principles through the whole tapestry of our lives, enhancing everything we do. I think you might agree that a good flirting encounter – one where both parties are relaxed and in the moment, with a hint of something exciting bubbling under the surface – is one of the best interactions we could experience. So why limit it only to the people we fancy? The same components that create a good flirting encounter – playfulness, a sense of being in the moment, a connection between two people, letting that other person feel as if they are seen and special – are elements that can (and should) be adopted into our daily lives and used with everyone. It's about connecting. As humans, isn't this why we are here?

This book is not just a 'How to' guide, it's also a 'How to be' guide – one that I hope will not just get you a partner, but take you wherever you want to go.

1

The Seven Biggest Myths About Flirting

FOLLOW ME DOWN this path and I know you won't regret it. Am I flirting with you? Perhaps, but I have some magic to show you . . . my magic formula. Over the course of the book, I'll be there to hold your hand as you take a long hard look at your goals and behaviour, and then at the world around you to identify who you are looking for and where you might find them. And then I will show you how to take this out into the real world. Scary? Oh no. Using Flirtology, this is the fun part – how to use my tried-and-tested system to cut through the complexities of the flirting world and get results.

First, though, I want to start by sorting out your current pre-conceptions about flirting. I've noticed that most people who come to me for help hold similar beliefs and have similar worries. The first step is to clear these away. Ready?

Myth 1: Flirting is difficult

Difficult: running a marathon, doing algebra, climbing Mount Kilimanjaro, solving the *Times* crossword . . .

Not difficult: asking someone a question.

Perhaps you don't regard asking someone a question as flirting. And this may be why you find the prospect of flirting so scary. It's either 'How *you* doin'?', as you surreptitiously flex your biceps or flutter your eyelashes . . . or nothing. So, since all the options either seem like bad stereotypes or over the top, you choose nothing. But the beauty of flirting the Flirtology way is that it starts from a simple question. Ask a question, then assess the situation: is this person responsive? Do they look like they want to engage? Do I want to continue engaging with them? Am I still enjoying this? Ask another question, then assess again. When you (or they) have had enough, make your graceful exit, and repeat with someone else. Flirting isn't like driving a Ferrari; you don't go from 0 to 60mph in less than three seconds. But the potential to flirt starts with a single question.

So, this is Principle One: **flirting is easy**. I give talks, workshops, seminars, flirting tours and coaching sessions on the science of flirting and the art of interaction. After it's over, the common response is, 'You make it sound so simple.' That's because the basics *are* simple. I understand that you might not believe me at this point, but bear with me. The reason it seems hard is because no one has ever taught you these basics; it's not something we are given a class on. (Which is a real shame.) The other reason it doesn't seem easy is because before we can address the basics, we must first strip away all of our assumptions, expectations, self-beliefs and extraneous emotions. This part, without guidance, is not as easy. But don't worry, that is what I am here for.

What does a great flirting encounter look like for you? Is it one where she sings the praises of your sparkling intellect? Is it one where you end up with his number? One where the two of you turn your corner of the party into a private world for an hour or two? One where you dazzle each other with your astonishing wit and extraordinary knowledge of *Game of Thrones*? One where you get a date (and not just a new Facebook friend)? Well, it can be any or all of these things, of course. But above all, a great flirting encounter is one where both yourself and the other person feel good. Both parties feel, 'Hey, this person gets me. This person can see me!' After all, this is what everyone is looking for: someone who makes them feel special, unique and seen. Think back to the last time you had a great flirt. Was it boring? Difficult? Awkward? No! A great flirting encounter is none of those things; more than anything else, flirting should be FUN!

Why do people want to flirt? I've asked this question in all sorts of frameworks – in my cross-cultural research, of my private clients, on my website – and I've received a variety of answers: 'I want to find a partner'; 'I want to go on more dates'; 'I want to be more confident with guys'; 'I want to ask a woman out without feeling awkward'; 'I want to feel more confident in social situations'. Towards the lighter end of the spectrum, flirting was 'a fun way to pass the time'. Sometimes it was even 'to see if I've still got it'. So, some people have specific end goals in mind while others are simply trying to give themselves a boost, to make themselves feel good.

The key point in all of this is confidence; confidence is about being happy to show others who you are. With this confidence comes ease. This is the state we are aiming for. What I have noticed over the last decade of helping people in this area is that the idea of expressing interest in someone you like turns the most confident and savvy person into a pile of mush. Almost all the clients who come to me have already told themselves they are '*hopeless at flirting*' or that they can't talk to strangers: '*People will think I'm weird or desperate if I approach them.*' Starting from this perspective, it's no wonder that the prospect of flirting feels more like a terrifying ordeal than a pleasure: you are dooming yourself to fail from the outset.

Later in this book, I am going to introduce to you the concept of the **mental model** and explain how harnessing it can be a powerful and positive tool. For now, think just about the following: what is your personal attitude towards flirting? Do you think you're good at it? Do you enjoy it? Do you think of it as a set of instructions you've got to follow or as a prescription for how you're meant to talk to people? Do you think you need to be dressed a special way or be in a particular place? Do you think there's a way of touching your hair or widening your eyes that is going to get results? Do you think there's an end goal that you must reach – getting the guy's number, getting some action, finding Ms Perfect?

Let's take the expectation down a few notches. You're not trying to find the great love of your life every time. You're not even necessarily trying to get a date. You're just trying to spark up a pleasing human interaction, one that might open the door to possibilities – dates, relationships, friendships, new experiences – or that might remain no more than an entertaining memory. So, above all, start to *believe*: you too can find all this enjoyable. And easy.

What is flirting to you?

1. Identify what you believe your current attitude towards flirting to be: Are you good at it? Shy? Awkward? Is each encounter a trial? A test? A joy?

2. Where do you think this attitude originated from? Your teenage years, your parents, your friends, an experience that happened to you?

3. Are you happy with this belief? Is it serving you well? Even if it used to serve you well, is that still the case?

4. What do you want your new attitude towards flirting to be?

   Some suggestions:

   - Flirting is fun and light.
   - It's just a flirt; it doesn't mean that I have to marry the person.
   - Flirting is about making both people feel alive.
   - I am not responsible for how the other person reacts to flirting.

5. Now, over the next month, notice whenever you are falling into your old pattern of only paying attention to

things that back up your first opinion. Immediately disengage. This time, only pay attention to 'evidence' that supports your new attitude. For example, if you go to a party and have fun flirting with a new guy but don't really think you are destined to be together, remind yourself of your new mantra: 'It's just a flirt; I don't have to marry the person.' You are free to enjoy the encounter for what it is. Or to bring it to a close without judging yourself.

Myth 2: Good flirts are born, not made

To recap the first point: flirting is light, it's fun, it's playful; it's not root canal surgery. And in theory this might sound great, if only there wasn't this little problem of you missing out on the flirt gene. Have no fear. The ability to flirt is not linked to biology. It's about human behaviour, and behaviour can be changed.

Principle Two: **flirting is a skill**. It can be learned. It can be taught. That's what I do. Not only can it be learned but, like any skill, it can also be improved upon with practice. Did you first sit down at the piano and immediately bang out a concerto? Did you first strap on some ice skates and begin twirling around the ice with ease? Why do we accept that we won't immediately become fluent in French, but we don't give ourselves the same leeway about immediately becoming fluent in flirting?

Just as there are artists who are amazingly talented from birth, so are there natural flirts who have built-in charisma. But most of us aren't Picasso, and most of us aren't astonishingly charismatic flirts. I promise that you won't need years of training to become a master at the art of flirting but, like anything else, it does require practice. As the golfer Arnold Palmer famously said, 'The more I practise, the luckier I get.' And, if you want, you too can learn how to get lucky . . .

It is true that in learning the skill of flirting you will be taken out of your comfort zone. You probably will feel awkward and self-conscious when you first start practising. I'm going to make you do things you don't normally do: walk up to strangers; smile at commuters on public transport; ask people questions which are more than a simple query about the time. There will be moments where you feel uncomfortable and like you aren't doing it 'right'. Just remind yourself that this isn't a failing on your part – it's to be expected. It's a logical part of the process of learning a new skill. And, like any skill, the more you practise, the more proficient you become. Flirting is no different.

It is by continuing to do things which make us uncomfortable that we become masters of them. I often hear from people that some of the things I ask them to do don't feel 'natural'. But what they really mean is that it feels uncomfortable.

And, yes, while at first it might feel 'unnatural' to be starting up conversations with people, if you did that every day for a month it would become part of your known behaviour. It, too, would start to feel 'natural'. Think about it like this: you're probably pretty confident in your job. You know what you're doing; you do it day-in, day-out. You know what to wear, you know which days your favourite food is served in the work canteen, and you probably even know if your boss is in a bad mood from the way they say 'Morning'. Were you born knowing all this? Is this a 'natural' phenomenon? No? So how come you're so confident about it now? The answer is practice. You have got to this point by doing the job eight hours a day for a long period of time. You not only know what to expect but you also know your own capabilities in the role. When it comes to the flirting world, you might get in one hour of practice every six months. It makes sense that you are unsure of what to do. Let's not eliminate the fact that because it makes you feel uncomfortable, you are probably avoiding it altogether and getting in zero practice. But what if you had spent eight hours a day flirting your little heart out? Do you think you'd feel more comfortable?

The interesting thing is that the majority of people feel they aren't good at flirting. Yet from my perspective as a flirting coach, I can see that everyone thinks *they* are the only ones who are like this, that the rest of world is made up of Marilyn Monroes and Casanovas, flirting from dusk to dawn and leaving men and women quaking in their paths. Let's look at things from a different perspective. Let's accept that most of us aren't comfortable with meeting new people, disclosing personal information to strangers and putting ourselves in a vulnerable situation where we might be rejected. Let's realize that we are just like everyone else in this arena. Then, with the understanding that the only way to improve is to practise, let's put ourselves in these uncomfortable situations, approach those good-looking, confident strangers, strike up those conversations that might lead who-knows-where. Let's learn this skill!

The challenge: ask someone a question

At the moment, your belief might be that talking to strangers will be awkward. This task is about recognizing that, with practice, we can get better at the things that make us uncomfortable.

The task: once a day, for the next week, ask a stranger a question

The guidelines:

1. You must make it clear that you are specifically asking the question to them. No general glancing in the direction of a group of people and mumbling something under your breath.

2. At this stage, all I'm expecting you to do is ask for simple information. You can start with something straightforward, like asking directions or asking the time. Your only goal here is to practise making contact.

3. Have no attachment to their part in the interaction. Your task is for you to ask someone a question. Your success or failure is not tied to their response but only to whether you completed the task or not.

4. It might be helpful if you set yourself a specific place or time like, 'Every morning on my way to work I am going to ask someone directions.' Oh, you mean you already know where you are going? Don't worry, remember the point of the task: it's to practise engaging with people in a simple way.

> 5. Avoid approaching: strangers in dark alleys, anyone muttering to themselves with a glint in their eye, or anyone wearing a Homer Simpson T-shirt, just because.

Myth 3: Flirting is frightening

I was 25 years old and teaching English in a small Japanese town an hour outside of Tokyo. My friends and I went into the city often to let off some steam in the famous Roppongi district. At a club one night, I saw an attractive man standing next to the dance floor. Due to his solo status and proximity to the dance floor, I thought he would be the perfect person for me to try out my new dance moves on. I walked up to him and said, 'Excuse me, would you like to dance?' He looked me up and down, shook his head no, and then looked away. My emotions revealed themselves in a range. First, I was stunned. I couldn't believe the harshness of his rejection. Then, as I walked back to my friends, I was very hard on myself: 'Jean, you're such a loser. You're so ugly. Why did you even do that?' Next was anger: '*He* is the loser. What a jerk! Why did he have to be such an ass about it? If he didn't want to dance, he could have said so in a nicer way . . .'

But after a few moments, I looked over at him and saw that he was now accompanied by another woman. I immediately felt better. 'Ah, he has a girlfriend. That's why he didn't want to dance with me. He was probably waiting for her and, when she arrived, didn't feel like explaining to her why he was dancing with someone else.' I decided that there is often a context that we don't know about. The other person could be tired, have bad hearing, be wearing very uncomfortable shoes, have a jealous partner waiting in the wings. We have no idea what is going on with them.

But the most important thing I learned from that night was about those initial few moments. Quite frankly, I am still shocked at how much abuse I gave myself due to this guy and his rejection. How could I let a complete stranger shake my self-worth like this? I didn't know this guy. He could be a puppy-kicking axe murderer for all I knew. He had already shown himself to not be the kindest of people. Why would I give this specimen the power to determine my self-worth? No one can do that except me. And from that day on, no one does. This is one of the biggest lessons that I have learned. When you allow your sense of self-worth to be influenced by strangers, don't be surprised when it doesn't go the way you want.

That experience happened almost twenty years ago, and I still think about it. It wasn't that I had ever been hugely lacking in confidence before, but that incident made me think about rejection logically, rather than at the gut-instinct emotional level which we usually operate on when someone turns us down.

And this is what leads to Principle Three: **flirting is not frightening**. Many people say they feel awkward going up to strangers and trying to start a conversation. Trying to think of something witty to say to impress someone you don't know, combined with the awkward feeling of doing something you're not used to, means that feelings of pressure can sabotage things before you even begin. Even worse, if you feel that by speaking to someone you are giving them the opportunity to make an assessment about you and giving them the power to accept or reject you as a person, then I can absolutely understand why the nerves might kick in.

But that is *not* what you are doing. You are not trying to think of the perfect thing to say to impress a stranger, not least because that is impossible. This person is *a stranger*, remember; you have no idea what will or won't impress them. Nor should you be using this moment as a chance to seek positive affirmation about your fabulousness from someone who doesn't even know you. You are asking them a question – nothing more, nothing less.

In the first instance, you are simply initiating, with the hope that it might turn into a nice encounter: that's all. **You are responsible for your part only.** You cannot predict nor control the other person. Let's not forget, you are dealing with a stranger here; you have no knowledge of them or their circumstances. They are a fellow human being, not the future father of your children, or your bride-to-be. Neither are they waiting, ready to weigh in on your looks, personality or all-round attractiveness. Instead, let's look at this interaction for what it really is: a short encounter with someone you'd like to speak to. And if they're not up for a conversation right now? Well, no harm done, move on. There could be a million reasons why they don't want to engage right now. Most of those reasons will have nothing to do with you. They might be busy; they might be married; they might have just received some terribly bad news or some terribly good news.

In other words, the reaction is all about them and has very little to do with you. So, why do we think that it does? In psychology, it's called 'the centre-stage syndrome': we always think we are on centre stage and everyone is watching us and judging us on our performance. In reality, no one is paying much attention to us. We are all just extras in the life performance of others. Once we stop trying to be the stars of their show, everything becomes easier. When you allow your sense of self-worth to be determined by other people, by the randomness of their ups and downs, baggage and moods, this is when flirting can seem hard. Do you really want to give this power to the random dude standing on the side of the dance floor in a nightclub in Tokyo? I did it once. Never again.

This frightening feeling is only possible when we look externally for approval, when we rely on others to make us feel good. I describe it as walking around with holes. Here's a hole: *'Hey, you, will you make me feel pretty?'* Here's another: *'You, you over there. I need you to make me feel safe and interesting.'* But what if we took care of those holes ourselves? If we filled ourselves up? If we didn't need to rely on the whims of others to do this for us? How would our feelings about flirting change if we thought about it in a different way?

And, anyway, let's examine these uncomfortable situations. How uncomfortable are they, really? What is it you are actually putting on the line?

On my Fearless Flirting tours, I often start off with a simple task: to go and make eye contact and then smile at three people. One particular time, a tour-goer came rushing back to me. 'Whew!' she said. 'That was a close one!' I was slightly concerned – what could possibly have happened? We were in an art gallery after all – not exactly a high-risk environment. 'My friend and I almost smiled at the same guy!' she said. I had to laugh. 'Er, why is that a problem?' I asked. 'Well, he would have surely thought we were crazy!' This scenario is not uncommon. People often worry that individuals have been smiled at more than once. No, it's not as life-threatening as it sounds . . .

This was the perfect moment to illustrate Principle Three. In cases like these, I like to turn subjective situations, which are always 'me' oriented, into objective situations, where one steps out of the immediate circle to have a look at what is going on with a more objective eye. I find that turning the tables is a helpful way to do that.

'OK, so if a guy and his friend both smiled at you, would you think they were crazy?' I asked her.

'Well, no,' she replied.

'And how would you feel if two guys smiled at you?'

'I would like it,' she said.

'Well then, why would you assume that he wouldn't like it as well?'

I've noticed that people seem to have two sets of rules: one for themselves and another for everyone else. In order to have a more objective viewpoint, we must have the same set of rules for everyone.

So, let's imagine the worst-case scenario here: the gallery-goer in question receives two smiles, from two women, and thinks they are both crazy. Well, why does this matter? That is his right. He doesn't know the women in question; he doesn't know their personalities, circumstances, hopes, dreams, ambitions. He doesn't have enough information to 'judge' them. In each flirting encounter, we are not laying our personalities on the line for judgement; we are not giving the other person the power to ruin our day if they don't say yes; we are not trying to find the great love of our life. You decide to smile, be happy, be kind to others because that is what you choose to do. That is how you want to be and how you want to live your life. This choice isn't dependent on other people.

Flirting is not frightening, because it doesn't involve handing the other person responsibility for your emotional well-being. Whether they enter into the spirit of the flirt or not is up to them. And if they choose not to, it is not a reflection on you.

Let's think about the gallery scenario again, in this light. What did the women in question have to lose? There was no question of 'failing' at this exercise. The task wasn't to smile at someone and get a smile back. It was simply to smile at someone. The only part we have control of. What the other person does with it is up to them. Maybe they'll be so surprised that someone smiled at them that it doesn't register until the next person walks by and they share the smile with that person instead. Maybe they return the smile to you and a great moment is exchanged. Or maybe they are not in the mood to receive a smile and do nothing with it. That is fine, because we don't give a smile to get a smile.

I have changed my own beliefs around this exercise over the years. I used to teach people 'How to start a conversation' but then realized that a conversation relies on the other person wanting to be involved; this is something that we don't have any control over and can't count on. So, now I now teach 'How to ask someone a question' – the only part we can influence. And the only way we can fail is if we don't do it. Failing is not linked to external factors, only to whether or not we followed through with what we wanted to do.

I like to think of a smile as giving someone a gift or a compliment. We wouldn't give these things with the intention of getting them back. It's the same with a smile. It's a chance to make someone feel good. And if they don't want to be made to feel good by us, we haven't been rejected; there's nothing to reject.

And that is why one of the principles of Flirtology is that flirting is not frightening: there isn't anything to be afraid of. Do you want your emotional well-being to hinge on the unresolved baggage, mood or self-development levels of every person you come across? No, didn't think so. You do what you want to do, and others will do what they want to do. Most of the time you will find that they are happy to receive your smile, and that will make it easier to give your next one. The point of this is that you maintain your own boundaries. You are responsible only for yourself.

And fear has another grip on us; it's usually linked to a tense that isn't real – the future. In the future, anything is possible, which means that we can be totally self-indulgent and let our brains run wild with speculation. If you are like most people, your attitude to making the first approach is probably something like, *'If I go up to someone, s/he will think I am crazy/desperate/pathetic.'* In the future tense, we can indulge ourselves to the utmost degree, thinking about worst-case scenarios that we are certain are bound to happen. We must not do that. Until the time that you have actually spoken to that person and he/she has laughed in your face, let's keep it real. Let's continually draw ourselves back to the only real place in space and time: the present. As one of my favourite people, Eleanor Roosevelt, once said: 'Yesterday is history, tomorrow is a mystery, today is a gift, which is why we call it the present.' Don't start writing scenarios out in your head. Don't start putting thoughts into other people's heads. Let them have their own thoughts, thanks very much. And if you see an opportunity to approach someone, step up there and take it. Don't think: just go!

 ## The challenge: give a stranger a compliment

Do you like it when people say nice things about you? (I really hope the answer is yes!) Do you think others would also like this? Then why don't you tell people nice things about them when they pop up in your head? When the woman with the gorgeous outfit walks by, why don't you say, 'I love your dress'? When the man with the intoxicating cologne is standing ahead of you at Starbucks, why don't you say, 'You smell nice!' When you are ordering your theatre tickets and the person on the other end of the phone is mesmerizing you with their dulcet tones, why don't you say, 'You have a wonderful voice. I didn't think ordering theatre tickets could be this enjoyable.' Say these things out loud when they pop up in your mind. Just as you like the unexpected compliment, so do others!

Withholding compliments for fear of being rejected or laughed at is the wrong approach. Making people feel good, in a genuine way, is a sure-fire way to make yourself feel good as well. Your task for the next week is to say one nice thing a day to someone. Here are a few guidelines:

1. It must be genuine.

2. It's best not to talk about any part of the body below the shoulders. (Except right thumbs. It's always fine to compliment someone's right thumb.)

3. Make the compliment as specific as possible. This allows the person to feel it in an even more personal way. For example, don't say, 'nice eyes', say, 'I don't think I have ever seen eyes as sparkly as yours.'

Myth 4: Rejection is a bad thing

Society teaches us that rejection is a soul-destroying experience, one that you must avoid at all costs. Even the fear of rejection, the hazy possibility that we might experience this gut-wrenching feeling in the distant future, is enough to stop us in our tracks. That is one powerful emotion! What if we looked at it in a different way, a way that didn't give it so much power? A way that showed off Principle Four: **rejection is one of the most powerful tools we have**.

When I was younger, my friends use to love introducing me at parties as 'the flirting expert'. And one of three things would happen with the guys at those parties: they would either 1) run a mile, 2) try to out-flirt me, like it was some sort of competition, or 3) take me into a corner somewhere . . . and turn me into an agony aunt, wanting my advice about some girl they liked. And people used to ask me in a very worried tone, 'Aren't you afraid of never meeting someone? Aren't most men intimidated by you?' My answer was no, I was not worried about never meeting someone. And, yes, some men were intimidated by me. It didn't bother me in the slightest. And the reason was that I knew rejection can also work as an effective weeding-out mechanism.

Anyone who was intimidated by me back in the day was never likely to be a good match. We might have fooled ourselves into it and tried very hard to be people we weren't to make it 'work'. But we could have never been happy together in the long term. I was looking for someone who could be an equal partner, self-confident and similarly independent, so if they rejected me on those grounds, they were doing both of us a great favour. Besides, at this point in your life, how many people do you think there are with whom you could happily share a tube of toothpaste, fold each other's laundry, make interior-design decisions for your living room, spend holidays with each other's families, live together pretty much 24/7? Do you think that number is going to be high? So then, why are we surprised when most people we meet wouldn't be a good fit?

When we find that we don't match with people, it's not a form of rejection. It's a gentle tap, pointing us in the right direction. It's not telling you there's something wrong with you; it's an effective mechanism to help you filter out those whom you fit with and those with whom you don't.

Compare these two statements, both taken from my research (these particular answers happen to have been given by Parisian males, but they reflect some worldwide attitudes).

The question was: 'How do you feel about rejection?'

One man answered like this: 'If you are rejected, it means you are not good-looking or you don't have a good personality.' Wow. That's quite a lot of self-doubt to take on from one short encounter.

Contrast this with another reply: 'I think, "At least it makes things clear." I move on to the next person. It helps me to get over her because I don't become obsessed with women who don't want me.'

Be honest – which statement do you find yourself agreeing with? And which do you think is most useful, constructive and likely to end in success?

In fact, it's worth giving the last word on this subject to another Parisian responding to the same question. How does this person look at it? Does he let rejection ruin his day? Does he let it eat away at his self-esteem? Absolutely not.

This is his answer: 'At clubs and bars, I'll say, "Hey, how's it going?" They say, "I'm not interested." It's not a defeat, because I did something nice, which people normally don't do. I give myself credit.'

Quite. And all of this leads me to the next important principle . . .

Myth 5: The perfect flirt can attract anyone

Picture this: you and a friend are going to a party. You're happy, you're looking great, you've had a good time getting ready, and you're hoping for an excellent night out. And if that involves a couple of flirtatious encounters, so much the better. Who knows, your next Mr Rights might be along at any moment. After a while, a man approaches your friend. He isn't really her type, but she politely laughs at his jokes (although, let's face it, bad puns are never really funny). He tells her all about his job as an accounts manager and, though it isn't in an area she's particularly interested in, she plays along and asks him questions and opens her eyes wide as he explains the finer points to her in great detail. When his favourite song comes on, she agrees to a dance even though it's not really her kind of music, and she finds herself spending most of the party on the dance floor with him, out of sync in every way. She is behaving in the exact same way as someone who actually *is* interested: laughing, asking questions and, most of all, still there. So, he's encouraged enough to ask for her number. And she gives it to him, hoping he won't ever call. But at least she knows she's still got it: someone out there is interested in her.

You, meanwhile, have your own evening going on. A second man approaches you. You give him a chance, but after a few moments of conversation it's obvious that you don't have much in common. He seems keen, but you politely disengage. You see someone across the room who takes your fancy and find a moment to approach him; you have a brief conversation, but it soon becomes clear he has a girlfriend, so you retreat. Throughout the evening, you circulate the party and talk to several guys, but none that you really hit it off with. Although you end up having a great chat with a girl you recognize from yoga class, you go home without any numbers; Mr Right clearly wasn't lurking at that particular bash.

Which of the two of you is the more successful flirt? You are. You might have gone home without any digits, but your friend got tangled up all night with someone she knew wasn't for her and now faces the prospect of trying to swerve a date without hurting his feelings. In the end, it was a waste of both of their time. But even worse than that, she has now made herself more susceptible to the sting of rejection. Using someone else as a means to help you feel good about yourself just reinforces your fear; it perpetuates a negative cycle in which you become more dependent on the positive affirmation of others, which in turn strengthens your fear of rejection.

Meanwhile, you made proactive decisions to speak with people of your choosing. There were no matches to be made that night, but it was by your own choice. You didn't feel the need to stick with the first person who showed any interest. And because you got in more practice of approaching people it means that you will feel more comfortable next time. When the right person does turn up, you'll be ready to enjoy the encounter.

This is Principle Five: **you don't have to attract everyone**. You have to attract the right people. How do you do that? Act like yourself, and you will attract people who like you. We all want to put our best foot forward, look our hottest, present our most clever selves in every flirtatious encounter. And we should. But there's no point in attracting people by presenting ourselves as something we're not. Laughing at jokes that aren't funny to us, feigning interest in subjects just so that we can convince ourselves we're popular – this is not what Flirtology is all about. Nor is it, I can assume, what you really want to be doing.

Flirtology is not about playing games or making up elaborate rules. It's not about pretending to be something we're not in order to chase down the next conquest. It's about authentically presenting ourselves as we really are. This means that you won't match with everyone. There will be knock-backs. That's absolutely fine – in fact, it's to be desired. Do you like playing sports? Nights out with your friends? Scandi crime thrillers? Then you don't have time to match with everyone! Remember, the list of potential applicants for this coveted position will not be high. It doesn't have to be – you only need one.

One of my clients was looking for a partner who was social and outgoing. She wanted someone who was interested in accompanying her to all of the events and parties that were an important part of her life. She was also very interested in reading and learning, and often spent time at her neighbourhood bookshop, which we pinpointed as a great place to start frequenting with an open mind and an alert eye. She told me she felt if she were to ask someone perusing the bookshelves, 'Have you read anything else by this author?', that he would probably be embarrassed, say one line and run away. Apart from the fact that she was falling into the trap of imagining an ending that hadn't even happened, I asked her why this reaction would be a problem. 'What if we looked at this in a completely different way? You've said how important it is for your future partner to find it easy to talk to people. If you were to ask someone in a bookshop a question and they didn't know how to respond and so ran off, would that person probably meet the coveted criteria of having fun going to events with you?

Therefore, would that person be a good partner for you? No. So, why not think of that as a way to effectively weed out those who wouldn't be a good match, and use it as a good starting point for those who would?'

We don't want everyone to be attracted to us. We want the people who are attracted to us to be the people we want to be with.

Myth 6: Men have to make the first move

Can women approach men? I get asked this quite a lot, and my answer is always the same: 'Of course.' And they should.

But you don't have to just take my word for it. On one of my recent flirting tours, a woman in her fifties asked me this million-dollar question. Rather than immediately sharing my (strong) view on the matter, I thought I'd open it out to the floor. In a mixed gender group, they were pretty much unanimous. This is Principle Six: **either women or men can make the approach**. In the words of one young man: 'Of course women can approach men. Who decided the roles anyway?' The ages of the people involved was significant here. The woman was used to things being done a certain way, and the younger man was used to things being less defined. I knew from my research into cross-cultural flirting behaviour that the majority of men liked it when women approached them, and they didn't think they were missing out on any kind of proverbial chase or that the woman was 'easy'. I often heard things like, 'Just because she has approached you, it doesn't mean anything. That's when the real game begins.' But I repeatedly find that most women don't know this to be true.

Why don't more women approach men?

Many women remain hesitant about making the first approach. Why? Well, lots of reasons are cited. I don't believe they are the real answers, but I do think it's worth examining them. The first takes us back in time. Up until about ten thousand years ago, human beings were hunter-gatherers. And, as the story goes, the men were the hunters and the women gatherers – the latter being the more passive role. Apparently, in 2018, men are still expected to take up this mantle, suggesting that they should hunt or approach women, who are in some sense their 'prey'.

Well, if we are to start taking our social cues from the behaviour of people who lived tens of thousands of years ago, we must first ask, is this story true?

A power dynamic between the sexes has been extracted from this example, but another important fact is usually omitted from the narrative: hunter-gatherer populations were highly egalitarian. Also, contrary to this neat and tidy storyline, women were also hunters. In India, 'The archaeological evidence shows that hunting involved women–men partnerships'. To take one modern-day example, the Aeta women of the Philippines are highly successful hunters.

And why is the 'man as hunter' storyline even relevant? There are plenty of other things we could have adopted from the hunter-gatherers such as a 15–20-hour work week, or animism as our main religious belief system. But we haven't. Why does this one feature seem to resonate so strongly with us?

The second reason cited for men to be the instigators of any encounter comes from an even more powerful fundamental source: biology. Broadly, it comes from the animal kingdom and revolves around the idea that this behaviour is 'natural'. Enter the chimp.

Chimpanzees are said to be the closest primate relative to humans, sharing 99 per cent of human DNA. Chimp societies are male-dominated, a relatively well-known fact. Using this example of male behaviour in the animal kingdom, the argument follows that human males are somehow also hard-wired to be the dominant instigators. But you might not have heard of our other close primate relative, also sharing 99 per cent of human DNA. They are the bonobos. Bonobos are a peaceful bunch, preferring sexual contact to violence. Promiscuity is encouraged, and there is little in the way of sexual behaviour that is off limits. Why don't we hear more about these primates? Well, unlike the case of the chimps, studies indicate that females have a higher social status in bonobo society. Highly sexed females? Running the show? Hmm, this doesn't really fit with the traditional narrative. Let's leave it out.

Most importantly, we are neither chimp nor bonobo but human. We have our own social structure. Why would we take our social cues from packs of animals who sleep in trees?

Men and women have more commonalities than differences. But we seem to be fixated on the few differences, blowing them out of proportion. These narratives are dangerous, as they paint women as passive, non-sexual and completely different from men. Even worse, many of us believe them without question.

But why do we accept these stories as fundamental truths? In my opinion, the answer is mostly an economic one. The reason that men asking out women has been the custom in the past is because the male members of our species, traditionally, have been the ones with greater access to money. This meant that they were responsible for having some form of transport to pick up the woman, often getting extra points for bearing gifts such as flowers or chocolates. They would also be responsible for paying the bill and ensuring the woman got home safely. As the woman would never be expected to open her wallet, this could be a pricey evening for the man. What did he get in return? Hopefully good company, the chance of another date, and perhaps some action of some sort. But his most prized luxury in all of this? Choice. He was the one who could choose whom to ask. All women could do was accept or reject the men who asked them.

But we no longer live in this world. While progress is sadly not complete, and women's earning power still lags behind men's, women today are approaching equality, and are certainly far more independent and wealthy than ever before. The old model doesn't have to hold sway any more.

We can actually see what the dating scene looks like in a culture that isn't tied to the notion that men need to make the first move. I went to Stockholm as part of my research on cross-cultural flirting behaviour. It is not a coincidence that in Sweden, a country where women make almost as much money as men, where women are strongly represented in politics and in business, where the state pays for things which are traditionally cost-prohibitive for women such as health and childcare, and where religion plays an almost non-existent role in society, there is a vastly different attitude to the question of gender roles and making romantic approaches.

I found that in Stockholm women are making the same choices that were traditionally only allowed to men. When it came to women approaching men, there was no debate. Everyone was all for it. I didn't hear a word about men as hunters or hard-wiring. One of the men I asked about this subject told me, 'Men and women are more equal in the flirting culture. There are no social codes about women not being able to approach guys.'

It's commonplace. As one guy explained, 'Guys are most likely to start looking at a girl, and girls are most likely to follow it up.' This is a far cry from what we are traditionally taught about gender roles, where the woman makes eye contact and the man comes up to her.

Another said, 'You respect women more; they are equals in the flirting arena. Women aren't that desperate. They don't even need to make the first move if they don't want. They can sit back and take it easy.'

I asked the men if they thought that women being economically independent has an impact on their flirting behaviour. One guy explained, 'Swedish women have more right to choose. They are more confident. In the States, there are so many rules girls have to follow, and they can be easily judged. In Sweden, girls can be as they want.'

And in another twist, one man said that Swedish women are worried about their reputation among their friends – they might be seen as gutless if they don't go up to that good-looking guy at the bar. Sound familiar?

We've all heard the spiel that men are 'visual creatures' who place more importance on looks than women do. As it turns out, women are also 'visual creatures' when they have the chance to be! Judging by the complaints of some of the Swedish male interviewees, they didn't much like the added pressure of being judged on their looks: 'The last decade has changed; with women becoming more independent it puts more pressure on men. We have to be interesting in other areas besides just providing food and money. In my father's generation, being a "good man" was enough; now we have to know about wine and art, be good dressers, etc. We have to be interesting and work harder on beauty. This is more obvious from the adverts. Probably because women demand it.'

Men of the world, do not let this worry you. Many of you already know the benefits of sharing the approaching role with women. Take it from the Swedish guys, the ones who know: 'It's an honour to be chosen'; 'I like a woman who knows what she wants'; 'It saves me a lot of trouble'. And, my favourite: 'I would rather be running with her than chasing her.'

The power to choose whom you want to talk to, go out with, sleep with and marry is something that should not be taken lightly. It is a form of self-determination that we should all be able to exercise.

Myth 7: The internet is the answer

As I've said already, in theory the digital world sounds like a perfect place to find a partner. No need to go out; you can make decisions on who would and wouldn't be a good match for you, whilst drinking delicious wine (without the expensive mark-up) in your pyjamas. But is convenience really the most important factor when it comes to finding something as important as love? Take, for example, the humble pizza. Why has anyone ever ordered a takeaway pizza (unless it's after the hour of 11 p.m., which is another story)? Is pizza that is delivered to your door ever the highest quality? Does it always come piping hot? Is it the most delicious pizza you can get? I think most of us would agree that to get the really tasty pizza, one must go to the place where it's made. So then why do we insist on having it brought to us, sub-standard as it is? Two reasons: 1) we love convenience; 2) we are lazy. And as far as pizza goes, of course it's fine to go with the convenient on occasion, even if it isn't quite as good. But why are we using the same mechanism to find our partners? 'Yes, I met John whilst lying on my sofa, perusing the menu. I chose a large, dark-haired guy with extra wit and hold the ego. He arrived at my door twenty minutes later. He's not exactly right, but I am too lazy to call and complain, so I just accepted the delivery.' If Kate Hudson is looking for her next blockbuster romantic comedy to star in, I think she should look no further.

This is the final principle, Principle Seven: **the answers to your dating problems do not lie online**. The issues with digital dating could run to a whole book by themselves, and I'll return to the subject later on. But briefly, here are some of the issues with it from a Flirtology point of view. First, we are offered an illusion: the illusion of endless choice. Approaching real live human beings as if they are a takeaway menu is a dangerous way of thinking. There is always the sense that there might be someone better out there; why go with door number 1 when you could also choose doors 2–5,222? Nearly one third of online daters already know this and agree that online dating keeps people from settling down, because there is always another option out there. This illusion of choice makes us picky. We think we can and will find someone who is better: 'That one was a bit too loud'; 'That one wore brown shoes and a black belt'; 'That one talked too much about her ex.' Instead of getting to know people as individuals, it becomes a game . . . next!

Second: dating sites offer filters, which, in theory, seem like a good idea. There certainly has to be some sort of mechanism to differentiate between all of these people. But they also give us a false sense of security – the filter will lead us to our perfect matches. I am a tall woman. When forced to make a choice, I would choose a tall man. My husband is short. In one tick, I would have swept away my wonderful partner. Choosing people based on a tick-box system carries the danger of eliminating people who might be brilliant for you, based only on something superficial. And, even worse, you can only look at categories that can be quantified: height, weight, income, age. And what one really needs to know about someone – whether they are kind, curious, have a good sense of humour or sparkling eyes – cannot be jammed into a box. Tick boxes force us to turn people into objects. There we are, classifying and quantifying other humans as if we were all rock collections. Oh yes, and it goes both ways; they are also doing the same to you!

And finally, the internet makes it all too easy to believe that you are really trying, that you are out there looking for people and throwing yourself into the dating scene. But are you? Does sitting behind a screen really count? Not in my book. Flirting is not just about the words you say or type; it's about the full package – the body language, the lingering glances, the back-and-forth, the electricity between you. Trying to recreate all that on the tiny screen of a phone is like playing with shadow-puppets. It's not really there.

What you are actually doing is giving your responsibility, your agency, over to an algorithm. Unfortunately, this is a bit like a gym membership. You can't just simply pay your monthly fees and magically become fit. You, yes you, need to own this. Your mighty screen will not save you from rejection. So, there's no point in trying to hide behind it.

However, with your new-found skills and your rejection-proof vest, you won't need a digital crutch. You've got Flirtology now. Ready?

2

Look in the Mirror:
Your Flirtatious Self

ARE YOU A good flirt? I'm talking about in the real world here; forget the likes and the retweets and Snapchat and Tinder banter, what I'm talking about is real-life, human, personal inter-action. One thing I often hear from my clients and audiences at my events is 'I'm hopeless at flirting'. It's not surprising, of course – it's one of the obvious reasons why people seek me out. But I often wonder what they actually *mean*?

For me, flirting isn't a separate activity that I do at specific times or locations; it's simply a way of bringing joy and cheerful-ness to everyday life. But if it doesn't come naturally for you at this point, don't worry.

Every conversation you have is practice, getting you into the habit of sparking up a human connection. My guess is that if you look at your own day-to-day interactions you will find that actually you do bring that element of the human and the humorous to quite a few of them; you just don't notice you're doing it. When you buy a newspaper from the friendly guy at the shop, do you cast your eyes at the counter and go silent when he gives you your change? Probably not. Do you in fact smile at him and make a cheerful comment about the dreary weather (I live in England; it's what we do). If the latter, then congratulations! You're a better flirt than you think.

But I can already hear your objections: that's not what you mean. What you think you are terrible at is flirting with intent – flirting to get a date, flirting to find a partner, flirting with someone you fancy. But why separate things out like this? Is it a better idea to go about 99 per cent of your life never flirting, and then in that 1 per cent space when you come across someone you fancy, to only flirt then? Gosh, that seems easy: 0 to 100 with no practice and the added pressure of being attracted to that person? On the other hand, if you have been sparking up your human connections in your daily life, it means that when you do stumble across someone you find attractive it won't be a big deal. It's just you again, having a human connection, but this time with someone who gets your pulse racing a bit. Flirtology is all about using the skills of flirtation in the real world, making real-life interaction into an art. And if this is your new normal, flirting with intent will now seem like a walk in the park. Well, a walk in the park where everyone is smiling and you go home with at least one attractive human's phone number.

Flirting style

Rather than thinking about whether you are a 'good' or 'bad' flirt, let's think instead about your flirting style.

At one end of the spectrum, there's the **non-flirt**. This person just doesn't participate in the flirting game; they go about their business, get from A to B and live their busy lives. They are no-nonsense and think that flirting is frivolous. They aren't often attracted to people, and there's no room for the extra hassle of trying to bond with every single person that they meet. And if their lives are full and they are happy, then no problem. Where it can cause a problem is when they feel that they would like to meet someone and want to make a connection. From a starting point like this, a room full of strangers doesn't look like a room full of possibilities; it looks like a room full of hassle. With this many people in the room, does this mean that there is going to be a huge queue at the bar?

Next, we have the **shy flirt**. This person could write a book about all the opportunities that have been missed due to being too afraid to make a move. They want to be able to talk to people. They want to make connections, but at the final hurdle they always find themselves doing nothing. They feel much more comfortable listening to others and waiting for them to make the move. But what happens when the people they are waiting for mistake their shyness for aloofness or their quietness as lack of interest? Their reluctance to proactively engage might make them feel safe, but is it giving them what they want?

In the middle of the spectrum is the **friendly flirt**. This person doesn't have much of a problem talking to people. They are good at cheerful chit-chat and don't mind passing the time of day with a stranger at the bus stop. It would never occur to them that what they are doing is flirting. What they find hard is how it all falls apart when they actually fancy someone. They can't handle the switch between seeming friendly and approachable to being sexy and alluring. For them, this isn't a spectrum; they are two separate skills. And that room full of strangers? Absolutely fine, so long as they're not trying to get a date with any of them.

Right at the other end of the spectrum is the **assertive flirt**. This person has game. They have no problem approaching, talking to and even flirting with people. Flirting with intent is no problem for them: they know what they want and how to get it. However, they don't always know exactly *who* they want; looking at that roomful of possibilities, they can find themselves going not for the person that will match them best but the person that flirts back with the biggest spark. And if they seem to be strongly flirtatious with everyone, then it's possible that their actual target will miss their signals. Or, with their big, extroverted personality, perhaps they are unintentionally stifling the other person – not letting them get a word in edgeways or not realizing that the 'me' show has gotten a bit repetitive. If they are constantly set to broadcast, not receive, then how can they let anyone else in? For them, a room full of strangers is a room full of fun. But what if they have had enough fun and are now looking for something more?

People seem to have this idea that the only people who need help with flirting are the non-flirts. And I have certainly helped many people who come to me with the attitude 'I just don't know how to do it'. The shy flirts make up the majority of the people who come to see me. If this sounds like you, rest assured that I have helped many a shy flirt transform from wallflower to sunflower. But extroverted flirts often find that they have problems too. They are flirting but never making connections. They are not making good choices, and they don't always get what they want out of their encounters.

Similarly, the friendly flirt can also have issues. We've already established that you probably do more 'friendly flirting' than you think you do. Which is a good thing: it's the Flirtology way. But where many people need help is the transition from friendly flirting to flirting with intent. If you're looking for results, rather than just a pleasant chat, you will need at some point to take that extra step. And that is what I am here to help you with. By the end of this book, whatever your starting point, you will have the tools to get results.

Quiz: what sort of flirt are you?

You see someone at a party who you find attractive. Do you:

1. Get another drink and go back to your friends?
2. Go over and introduce yourself with a warm handshake?

3. Glance over a few times and hope they come over to you?

4. Start with some eye contact and then sashay over with an inviting smile?

The cute barista at the coffee shop gives you a compliment with your latte. Do you:

1. Pretend you don't hear, take your coffee, and go?

2. Give a smile and say, 'Thanks very much!'

3. Look down, give an embarrassed laugh and scurry off?

4. With a lingering look say, 'And I could say the same for you . . .'?

Upon entering a crowded bar, do you:

1. Walk in; it's a bar?

2. Have a swift glance around as you make your way to your friends?

3. Spot your friends and put your head down until you reach your safety net?

4. Walk in as if everyone's watching, while scanning the room to see if anyone's watching you?

You see someone on your morning commute to work who is cute. Do you:

1. Continue reading the paper so that you appear to be too busy to notice?

2. Give them your newspaper and say, 'I'm done with this, would you like to read it?'

3. Peek up once or twice from your paper when you think they are not looking?

4. Make eye contact several times. Once you notice they are reciprocating add an alluring smile?

If you got mostly 1s – you are a non-flirt. Flirting doesn't seem to factor in your life. You might be missing out on some incredible connections and good fun.

If you got mostly 2s – you are a friendly flirt. You are off to a good start here. It's nice to be nice, but do you always want to be the friend? You need to add in some flirtiness to your encounters.

If you got mostly 3s – you are the shy flirt. You are missing out on countless opportunities for both making friends and getting dates by being afraid. Flirtology will show you how to get over your fear.

If you got mostly 4s – you are an assertive flirt. You are not shy and don't miss much. That's wonderful. You go in all guns blazing and usually get what you want, for the short term at least. Let's make sure that you are not missing potential partner opportunities.

Goals

Regardless of what type of flirt you are, if you want to use Flirtology to enhance your love life, the first thing to establish is your goals. Beyond the social lubrication and general life-enhancing qualities of flirting, you may be thinking that you want to use

Flirtology to meet more new people, to go on more dates, have more sex or to find The One.

Only you can know exactly what your goals are. However, there are three things I would encourage you to remember:

1. Goals can, and do, change. Think about what's right for you *right now*, not some vague long-held wish that may come true one day. Many people come to me saying they are looking for a long-term relationship. (This is not a surprise. It's what society has conditioned us to do from an early age: 'Pair up! Procreate!' Do we ever hear the message: 'Explore! Meet lots of people! Learn more about yourself!'?) Quite often, once people have looked at their lives properly they come to the conclusion that at this particular moment what they actually need is quite different. Is this you? Only you can tell. But be honest with yourself.

2. Don't take on other people's goals. Just because everyone else in your friendship group is thinking about houses, cars, mortgages and getting married, it doesn't mean you have to too.

3. A goal is just a marker which focuses your attention. Once you have set a goal, release it. We usually don't have control over our final goals, because reaching the goal involves more people than just us. For example, your goal is to get a raise. Can you alone achieve that? No. It depends on your boss, and maybe even her boss. To castigate yourself when you don't achieve a goal because more people than just you

are part of the process is foolhardy. And so is being frustrated that you want to be in a relationship and aren't in one. It takes more than you alone to achieve this goal. Focus on what you do have control over: each little action step. And while it might seem small, each step puts you closer to your desired result.

But it is true that many people come to me because they are looking for a relationship, so let's assume that that might be one of your goals. It may well be why you're reading this book. You're single, and you don't want to be. How can you change that? Let's look at it from a properly researched Flirtology point of view.

Establish your goals

First, *set out* your goals. When people come to me for coaching, I ask them first to fill in a simple form. The questions are not complex, but it is important to set the answers down in black and white. The reason for this is that people are often quite fuzzy about what they are actually trying to achieve. Writing goals down forces you to confront what you are looking for. These are the questions I ask them:

1. What is the main thing you are looking to get help with? Are you looking for a long-term relationship? For more confidence? To become better at flirting? To widen the pool of people you meet?

2. What do you think is holding you back?

3. Please name three specific goals that you have. Per-haps being comfortable going to parties; making new friends; going on several dates a month.

Second, *interrogate* your goals. Why do you think you want these things right now? Does it fit in with what you want in the rest of your life? How do your answers to question 1 chime with your answers to question 3? If what you are looking for is to meet more people, what can you do immediately that will help you achieve that? Is this what you should be focusing on to start with? Is that what you have written down?

Third, *refine* your goals. Look at the list of questions again. Are there any changes that would make them more effective and achievable?

Obstacles

You've set your goal. You've established, say, that you want to find a partner. But you're still single. What seems to be the problem? Besides the fact that your goal involves the cooperation of more people than just you, there's another issue: your obstacles. You see there is a problem, but you can't seem to fix it. In our modern-day lives, we can fix most things in an instant. We're hungry – we use a food-delivery app. We're bored – we look at our phone again. But when it comes to finding a partner for a happy relationship, we can't seem to 'fix' this. So, we use our brains and ask ourselves why. Why is this happening?

At my talks, I often ask the audiences what they think the problem is with their love life. And after years of doing this, I can tell you that the answers to this question always fall into two distinct categories:

1. It's everyone else: there's something wrong with other people. This is what I call an **external excuse**. This covers a raft of reasons: I live in a city, it's unfriendly. I live in the country, there's nobody to meet. The people I meet are only interested in being friends. The people I meet are only interested in one-night stands. The people I meet are the wrong sex/age/type of person. The external excuses are circumstances in your life which you think are just a fact of your life and beyond your control.

2. It's me: there's something wrong with me. This is what I call an **internal excuse**. It's my location; it's my lifestyle; it's my wonky nose; it's the fact that I was brought up with only sisters, so I don't know how to talk to men. Internal excuses are your personal and individual circumstances that you feel make it uniquely impossible for you to find someone.

Left to our own devices, we come up with a plethora of reasons why things aren't working. We then feel reassured because we have figured out the 'problem'. And because the problem never involves much wrong-doing on our part, it also means that we don't have to change our behaviour: it's not really our fault. And then we are trapped, unchanging, doomed to continue making the same mistakes, all the while placing the blame for our continued circumstance somewhere else.

Well, let's look at these excuses and deal with them rationally.

External excuses

First off, let's look at the external excuse. The fact is, sometimes this excuse is valid. There are some circumstances which do make it difficult to meet people. It is possible that you are living in a small remote community and that new faces are few and far between. Or that you work nightshifts and time for socializing is severely limited. But it is rare to have circumstances that completely prevent you from finding a good flirting partner. Much more often, the external excuse is a story that you have got used to telling yourself. Something you unquestioningly accept as fact and allow to interfere with your goals.

The external excuse is too often nothing but a recycled myth. I happen to live in London, which is a place that seems to glory in its reputation for frosty reserve. But scratch beneath the surface of that reputation, and it soon begins to fall apart. The city may be busy and fast-paced, yes, and it may have its share of bustling commuters intent on their busy lives. But is it likely that *every single* Londoner is unfriendly? Not at all. Similarly, you might hear over and over again that there are no decent men out there or that all women are only interested in men with flashy jobs. Again, is this really likely? (And if it is, perhaps you should think about the kinds of circles that you move in.)

Rather than accepting this kind of lazy labelling, I want to encourage you to interrogate it. Not just to question what you hear others saying around you but also to take a clear and object-ive look at your own observations and beliefs. This is where methods derived from social anthropology can really help you.

1. First, think about your **key informants** (key informants are those people whose social positions in a culture give them specialist knowledge). When you hear yourself repeat a generalized negative 'fact' such as 'people aren't friendly' or 'there are no decent men out there' ask yourself the follow-ing questions. Who is my source? Is it a sort of cultural hearsay, something that people repeat without thinking? Is it a media trope or cliché, such as 'You're more likely to get struck by lightning than meet a man once you're over the age of 30'? When you state with such confidence that no men out there are interested in a serious relationship, does this perhaps come from your friends – who may well be in different circumstances to you or have their own bag-gage which they are projecting on to you? Or does it come from the kinds of magazine you read or the movies you have watched? In other words, are your key informants reliable?

2. Perhaps you will say that no, what you are saying reflects your own personal lived experience in the real world. You know London is unfriendly because you take the tube every morning: have you ever seen so many grumpy, irri-tated faces? You know that there are no decent men out

there because you go to bars and have had the meat-market experience too many times.

This is where the crucial principle of **sample size** comes into play. This is a key concept in social anthropology, and it asks what you are basing your observation on. What is your evidence? How many times has this negative experience actually happened, and what were the conditions? Are there any other possible explanations than the conclusions you have drawn?

If you look at it honestly, are you allowing a couple of sleazy bar experiences to colour your attitude not only to nightlife but to an entire gender? Are you taking people's demeanours in the middle of a stressful commute as a guide to their actual personality? And proceeding to label an entire city?

3. Negative experiences tend to stand out to us, living in our memories in a way that can distort our perceptions. Called the **negativity bias**, the power of negative experiences is actually meant to help us, from an evolutionary point of view. The risks of responding inappropriately to negative events are greater than the risks of responding inappropriately to positive events, since negative events can, potentially, kill us, while positive events will merely enhance our well-being. As wonderful as this inbuilt trait might have been for our ancestors when deciphering between poisonous and edible plants, when it comes to our experiences of modern daily life, this negativity bias is often more of a hindrance

than a help. It can work to keep us trapped by giving the negative experience undue significance.

If you are extrapolating negative lessons from a handful of encounters, then ask yourself whether you have really tested your assumptions over time, in multiple instances. Have they always proved to be the case? If not, then don't take them as 'truth'. We often draw conclusions that aren't backed up by evidence.

The age question

There is one particular external excuse I hear so often that it needs to be examined carefully. I often hear: 'Once you are a woman older than her late thirties, dating becomes impossible. There is nobody out there to meet.'

I celebrated my twenty-sixth birthday in Japan. And, after wishing me a happy birthday, a Japanese male teacher explained that I was now a 'Kurisumaskekki'. Noticing my bafflement, he explained the theory: Japanese attitudes to the ideal female marriage age can be compared to the stages of popularity a Christmas cake goes through. Now that I had passed the magical 25th, I wasn't fresh, my value had declined, and half-price was the best I could expect. Great.

But apparently there has been progress. I was recently reading an article in *The Economist* about an unmarried woman now being a 'New Year's noodle'. The theory being that many Japanese spend 30 or 31 December eating soba noodles. Thus, this theory claims women reach their peak marriage value at 30 or 31 years old. However, as these are 'noodles to pass the year', once a woman hits 32 her value will plummet.

So, it looks as if in the 18 years since I lived there, a Japanese woman has gained a good six years of singledom before she is considered an expired food item. That's progress.

We might laugh at this, but if you're a woman in her late thirties, that laughter could be slightly strained. Sometimes things don't seem much better wherever you are in the world.

The theory in the UK goes as follows: once a woman hits her late thirties, it's hard for her to meet anyone of her own age because all the men out there are either taken or only interested in younger women. Or simply don't exist! (Men in the 35–50 age demographic are an urban myth, obviously.) The irony is that I know there are men in this demographic reading this right now silently screaming, 'I'm here! I'm here!'

So, what's the truth of this? Well, the first thing I will say is that if you have shrunk your frame of reference down into the *online* dating world, you may be on to something here.

Some rather off-putting online dating stats: in the virtual world, a woman's desirability peaks at 21. By 26 she will still have more online pursuers than men. But by 48 the tables have turned. Men now have twice as many online pursuers as women.

But the great joy is that in the real world, people don't filter in the same way that they do online. In the real world, we can't just block people out of our field of vision because of a figure they have entered into a box on a form. The man who, in his online avatar, is checking the box that says he wants 21–30-year-olds may in real life be beguiled by the killer moves of that 39-year-old on the dance floor. And the woman of 45 who is only searching for men in her age bracket or older? Who is to say that she won't find fascinating conversation in someone who turns out to be ten years younger than she thought? In other words, who says you have to date people of a certain age?

And in fact, as many male readers will know, it's not just women who get pressured about why they are single. A recent male client came to me saying he felt guilt and shame about being single. To him it was a problem that needed 'fixing'. At 45 years old, he felt constant pressure from those around him saying things like, 'C'mon, it's time to sort yourself out now' and 'Why are you still single? What's wrong with you?' Let me ask you, how easy do you think it is to find someone if you are operating under a cloud of guilt and shame?

Recently I had a private client, a woman in her mid fifties. She came with the firm opinion that there are no decent single men in her age group. She told me she had tried everything, and most of the men she met that were her age were 'dweebs'. I asked her if she thought the process of finding a partner was hard, and she said, 'Yes, very.' Her headline story was the familiar one: 'EXTRA! EXTRA! DATING IS HARD WORK: THERE ARE NO GOOD MEN OUT THERE OVER 50!'

As usual, after speaking with her a bit more, it turned out there was more to the story than the headline that she had been flashing. In fact, she *had* been happily dating a man in his thirties but had gotten so much grief from her adult children that she stopped seeing him.

Next, she told me that she had to be careful about whom she

dated, as she has a close social circle and didn't want to upset the apple cart.

Then she admitted that there had been a few times where men in their forties had expressed interest, but she thought that they couldn't possibly be interested in her.

So, on closer inspection, what was limiting her dating possibilities? Was it a complete lack of men out there? Clearly not. Was it perhaps a series of barriers that she was putting up in her own mind? A combination of pressure from others and her own self-doubts? It seemed she was the one limiting her choices. As I explained to her, she had put up so many walls, there was no room left for an actual person.

In another example, a private client of mine also in her fifties came with the same excuse. After doing a few coaching sessions together, it turned out that her underlying belief was that no one who could be an equal partner would actually be interested in her. Which is why she was under the impression that there weren't any 'decent' men out there in her age group. She kept going for the ones who weren't a good match for her, with the belief that she wasn't good enough. After we identified these mental models, it turned out that there were some good men who were already in her life, who had been showing interest, but she just wasn't open to it. She is now happily dating her spin instructor, one of these guys who had been interested in her all this time.

The lesson? If you are a woman caught in this seemingly intractable age dilemma, change your focus. First, **get off the internet**. Second, **look at your own behaviour**. Third, allow yourself to **broaden your horizons**. You don't have to find a man who fits into a certain set of narrow boxes: age, career stage, social status. There are people out there – of all ages – who won't be sizing you up as though you are an item of grocery shopping. And if you ever consider comparing yourself to a stale cake or a bowl of noodles: don't. You are a human being.

Internal excuses

But what of the internal excuses, the ones where you believe your bad luck has everything to do with you and your own unique circumstances? These can feel even more insurmountable. They are personal, after all. They are going on inside you.

This is something I have seen repeatedly. If people feel, for example, that speaking to women is hard, they will scan their brain trying to think of reasons why. They'll think of all of their life experiences, past histories, and then come up with what seems like a logical explanation to them. 'Aha, the reason that I find it difficult speaking to women is that I went to an all-boys school, so I didn't learn how to interact with women in my formative years.' Little do they realize that, other than James Bond, most men find it difficult walking up to a woman cold and starting a conversation with her. Incidentally, every male client that I've ever had was under the impression that every other guy had no problems walking up to women and beginning conversations.

So, what to do about these seemingly indelible opinions you hold about yourself?

1. The first thing to remember is **the only life experience you really know is your own**. You have no idea how easy or difficult things are for everyone else. You simply don't know what things feel like from anyone else's point of view. (Pssst – if you haven't figured it out by now, people's Facebook feeds aren't exactly the most accurate representations of their lives.) Just recognizing this is powerful, so try not to get hung up on comparisons – an easy trap to fall into.

2. The same process applies to internal excuses as to the external ones: consider where you are getting your opinions. Once more, you need to think about your **key informants**. Who are the people that you talk to about your problems? I have found that people carry around unquestioned distorted views of themselves based entirely on things said to them by friends, siblings or parents. (You would be amazed at the kinds of distortions people have acquired from their mothers in particular!) Usually, these key informants don't mean to be harmful but, unintentionally, they help propagate unhelpful myths. Often, they are carrying their own baggage and burdening you with it too. A female client once came to me after deducing that she was too independent and wouldn't ever be able to fit someone else in her life, even though she wanted a partner. This was making her doubt whether she could ever sustain a relationship. After talking it through, it turned out that this 'fact' derived from a story that her mother relayed to her about when she was a young child. She didn't even

remember the incident happening. It was second-hand, filtered through her mother, and it was greatly affecting her life and happiness over 30 years later!

I once had an American client in her late forties, a very attractive person who was always beautifully dressed and looked fantastic. But in talking to her about why she thought she was having trouble meeting someone, she came up with the 'fact' that it was harder for her now that she was older, because she wasn't as attractive as she used to be. 'Hang on,' I said, 'do you really believe that?' She stopped, and looked like it was the first time that she had ever truly considered it; her expression completely changed. 'No, I don't think that, actually. I think I look better than I did when I was younger.' 'Well then, why are you holding on to this belief?' I asked. It suddenly dawned on her that the reason she had assumed her looks were going had nothing to do with her appearance at all. It was because she frequently got together with two particular girlfriends, and the main topic of conversation was how they were all getting older and less attractive. These friends hadn't *meant* her to feel less good about herself. They weren't telling her specifically that she was ageing horribly. But subconsciously she had taken this completely erroneous 'truth' on board and allowed it to colour her thinking. Had she happened to spend time with people who were happy in themselves, her attitude to herself would have been completely different.

3. Not all negative perceptions come from other people. The most powerful ones come from within: '*I can't talk to people I'm attracted to*'; '*The people I fancy won't think I'm good enough for them*'; '*I'm not attractive enough for that person*'. These are all examples of a very powerful concept in this book: the **mental model**. This is the third key to tackling internal excuses. What does this mean? It's worth looking at in detail.

Mental models

So, what are mental models? They are the lenses through which you view situations. I was first introduced to the concept of mental models by Srikumar Rao, a speaker, author and former business-school professor. This concept has played a very important part in my teachings, and I would like to thank him profusely. The concept goes like this: as individuals, we all have mental models about many sorts of different things – our attitudes towards our siblings, our feelings about ourselves, and even the way in which we view the world (is it a good place or a scary place?). Out of all the information floating through our consciousness, we pick and choose the small amount of material that fits with our models and disregard the other 98 per cent. This 'evidence' strengthens our models and reinforces them as our reality.

The models are neither good nor bad; our lenses are no more real or unreal than anyone else's. It's not a problem that we have mental models; it's natural. The problem arises when we don't recognize that we are simply viewing a situation through a model – just one of many ways of filtering the world – and instead believe that the way we see things is *the truth*.

Let's look at how your mental model is the basis from which all of your outcomes derive:

- You hold in your head certain thoughts.
- These thought models affect your behaviour.
- Your behaviour affects what actually happens – the outcome.

Not only are your outcomes directly linked to your mental model, but the mental model also has the capacity to become a self-fulfilling prophecy.

Let's take a really common example: '*I can't talk to people I find attractive.*'

You might not have consciously recognized it yet as a 'mental model', but your current attitude to the idea of talking to a woman you find attractive at the bar might go something like this: '*I don't mind talking to strangers generally, but if I go up to that woman and start speaking with her, I'll say something stupid or struggle to find the right words. She'll know I fancy her, and she'll think I'm creepy. It will end in embarrassment, and I'll feel terrible.*'

Despite all this, you are trying to be brave and proactive, so you muster the nerve to go up to her anyway. You become more and more apprehensive as you approach, and your mind chatter is in top gear: '*This is bound to go wrong. There's no way she's going to want to speak to me. This is going to be so awkward!*' Sure enough, when you find yourself beside her you tentatively try to get her attention, your body language showing you are poised for flight the whole time. When she turns to speak to you, you realize you haven't thought about what to say beyond clichés, so you stammer something that feels really inappropriate. So half-hearted is your attempt that at first she's not even fully sure it's her you're talking to. She doesn't bat you away, but she doesn't look that enthusiastic or turn around to engage with you properly. Your rehearsed conversational gambits hang in the air. After a while, you awkwardly mutter that it was nice to meet her, and retreat. You leave the bar crestfallen, your expectations reinforced: you are terrible at this and can't talk to people you fancy. You reassure yourself that you won't be trying that again in a hurry! The fact that your behaviour did as much as anything else to achieve these results doesn't cross your mind. The fact that at every step you were sending her messages both through your body language and your tone of voice that she shouldn't talk to you doesn't even factor into your conclusion. Nope. That's how the mental models, and the negative bias, keep you trapped.

You must, for a moment, recognize that not *everyone* has that same fear about talking to attractive people. Some people even seem to enjoy it, I hear! So, what are they doing differently to you? The difference lies in their different mental model. Their mental model might be: '*It's fun meeting new people.*' Therefore, they might see this same woman and think, '*She looks attractive. I wonder if she's also good fun. There's only one way to find out: I'll go and talk to her.*' This means that their behaviour is different. Rather than hesitating long enough to allow doubts to creep in, they act immediately. They treat the attractive stranger like they would anyone else, approaching with a friendly demeanour and with an idea of a question to ask but without a forced and cheesy line. They'll come across as natural – after all, their entire self-worth isn't on the line. They are simply checking out if this person is as fun as she appears. Maybe the woman will respond positively, maybe she won't. But they may well have a minute or two of conversation. And at the end of the encounter their basic belief – that it is fun meeting new people – is reinforced.

So, what if you change your mental model? You will have to choose one that resonates with you, but perhaps it could be: *'It's nice to find out about people.'* Or *'Most people are happy to talk, just like I am.'* This has a knock-on effect. You don't start imagining her reaction or worrying about what a knock-back might do to your self-esteem. If you approach her with the mental model of *'It's nice to find out about people'*, then the encounter would be more about simple curiosity: *'I wonder what she's like?'* Approaching her in this spirit would allow you to be more natural, and you would feel no pressure. Isn't this the goal?

Your opening gambit might not be a cheesy chat-up line but an attempt to work out if you're going to have anything in common. This creates different behaviour: your conversation is natural, your body language open, your approach doesn't seem forced. And she may or may not want to get into a long conversation, but your original aim was simply to find out if she was fun or not. If not, it's no reflection on you.

The magic here is that changing your mental models changes your behaviour, and this in turn changes the outcome.

- It starts with a thought in the mind: 'Life is good!'
- The thought affects my behaviour: I smile.
- This, in turn, affects the outcome: someone smiles back at me.
- My mental model is confirmed: life is good!

Possibilities not problems

Think about the mental models that govern your flirting behaviour. Ask yourself if they are helpful. The chances are that if they are causing you discomfort, then they are not helpful.

Often the mental models will involve a negative attitude towards yourself, but not always. Sometimes the mental model is something you deliberately tell yourself, mantra-like; something that feels like a strength rather than a weakness. For instance, *'I have high standards; I'm not going to settle for someone who isn't perfectly right for me.'* And nor should you.

But have a think about what this statement is doing to your behaviour: are you walking around with a mental checklist, assessing each potential partner that you meet against it? Does it make you open and curious, ready to talk to anyone and everyone to see what you have in common? Or do you find it shutting you down, preventing you from engaging with people on even a very basic level because they haven't matched up to an imaginary set of standards?

Examining mental models is key to challenging those ingrained internal excuses you are walking around with. *'I can't find anyone because of my lifestyle/upbringing/job/family circumstances'*: these are all unhelpful mental models, and it is up to you to examine them and change them for something that will add value to your life.

'*My career is too demanding. I don't have time to meet anybody*' might become '*I've really achieved good things in my career. Now I'd like to find ways of taking that success into my social life too.*'

'*I'm too shy to meet new people*' might become '*I wonder where I might find people who share my interests and with whom I'll feel comfortable.*'

So, the next time you hear yourself think '*I can't meet anyone because . . .*', check yourself. Instead of getting locked into the same tired excuses, both internal and external, free yourself from these thoughts. Here's a simple antidote: ask yourself these questions instead – are there any other possibilities as to why this is happening? And then – how can I make them work for me and not against me?

Traps

Once you have challenged your own excuses in this way, the landscape suddenly looks different. But you still might not find yourself achieving your goals. Why is this?

There are all sorts of traps that we could be falling into, that can significantly affect our chances of having great flirting results. Here are just a few that you might recognize in yourself:

1. **Over-busy syndrome.** One of the most common things I hear from clients is that they never meet anyone even though they are always out. They will assure me that they

are doing all they can, but when I dig deep into their lives, I discover that they are working dawn till dusk, stopping off at the same gym and the same sandwich place and never talking to anyone. But they make time for a really active social life, they tell me. So, I ask more questions about what this means. It turns out that they are going to a restaurant, with a different friend, once a week. Which is lovely. But sitting in the corner having involved catch-ups with friends is not the best way to set yourself up for those all-important flirting opportunities.

2. **Missed-opportunity syndrome.** A very common habit is to put flirting and dating into one tiny compartment in your life – something you do once a month, on a big night out, with the help of tequila. You are only open to meeting some-one and flirting on a certain date in the diary, at a certain venue, wearing a certain outfit. Why is that? The Flirtology way is to weave the spark and joy of flirting into every area of your life, so it follows that opportunity can knock at any time – in the supermarket, at the gym, on your commute . . . Change that mental model, the one that says the only appro-priate place to flirt is when you are dressed in your best and on a night out. Flirting can happen anywhere.

3. **Rom-com syndrome.** I blame Meg Ryan. Too many peo-ple are carrying around in their head the perfect 'meet-cute' scenario, believing the moment they meet their future partner will come with bells and whistles. It will be a hilar-ious story they'll tell their future children, it will be

significant in some way. Not often true. It's much more likely that the first conversation you have with your future beloved will be banal and forgettable. It's not the first conversation that matters, though . . .

4. **The Mr/Ms Perfect syndrome.** 'There's nobody out there . . .' Often this translates as 'there's nobody out there who fits the ever-narrowing criteria you have fashioned for yourself'. Well, yes, if what you are after is a fun-loving and carefree yet hugely successful executive exactly five years older than yourself; tall, dark and handsome, with no baggage and a creative side plus a sense of humour, then it might be rather difficult to track them down. If, on the other hand, you widen your focus to include people whom you enjoy spending time with, then you might find them suddenly popping into view.

5. **The project-management syndrome.** Another way we try to fix this 'being single' problem is by having a plan and investing every extra waking moment into that plan. One of my clients has a high-powered position in the City. She has moved her way up the ranks by being ambitious, good at strategy and at implementing that strategy. In her work life, this has paid off. She is trying to employ the same strategy to solve the problem of being single, and it's not working. She first came to me, showing me her 'find a partner' strategy. Of course, it was written down. I am sure there were diagrams. I said, 'Hey, how are you feeling?' She looked at me, 'Quite frankly, I am exhausted.' Finding a

partner for love can't be carried out in the same way one would a work merger.

There is one thing that unites all these traps: they are all to do with your own attitude. That is, each of them is tied up with a *belief* you hold to be true – a mental model that gets in the way of your natural ability to engage. What these obstacles have in common is that they are all in your head.

And that's the good news. Because if they are all in your head, you have the power to get rid of them. These traps are under your control. Discard them, change them, and who knows what might happen?

How to be attractive

Perhaps the most prevalent trap of all is the fear that somehow we aren't attractive enough. The reason we can't go up and talk to that person over there is because, physically, we don't think we measure up. If only we were slightly taller, thinner, better looking . . .

For years, I played 'the attractiveness game'. I wore dresses, make-up, my nails were always manicured, my hair was long, often blonde. I restricted my calories and worked out like a fiend. I played my part brilliantly and was well rewarded. Things have changed.

It's summer as I write this, so of course I am taking frequent breaks to consume my Ben & Jerry's ice cream. In the past, it would have been frozen yoghurt. I find the easiest and most pleasurable way to get around my city is by bicycle, not the most conducive for dress-wearing, so they are saved for special occasions. I wear little or no make-up now, most of it natural and organic; I've stopped wasting (as I see it) precious time and money having people paint toxins on my nails. As for my eating habits, I've stopped restricting and started enjoying. I can't believe that I hadn't eaten pizza in almost ten years! And whilst I still enjoy exercise, instead of hard-core circuits, hoping for a firm ass and toned abs, it's now about things that make my body *and* soul feel happy: yoga, Pilates and walking. The quest for a thin body just isn't part of my mentality any more. This new attitude is a drastic change from the one encompassing the last 20 years of my life. And it hasn't arisen because I have now found a partner. Rather, it's from watching and questioning what I see around me. I refuse to play the game any more. Am I still attractive?

What does it mean to be attractive? Looks-wise, society presents a specific model for us to follow: just look a certain way and good fortune will follow. But how accessible is that model for most people? And, more importantly, what happens if you can't physically measure up to it? If, for example, something pesky called genes have gotten in the way? Eighty per cent of our height is pre-determined. Most people accept that there is not a lot they can do about it. What percentage of our weight is determined by genes? According to scientist Dr Traci Mann, it's 75 per cent. I think of the woman I see at the gym: she looks great but never feels happy with her body. 'I need to lose more weight!' she says every time I see her. And while there is a little wiggle room for a change in our physical bodies, it's so much less than we accept.

And I can see why some people, like the woman at my gym, don't want to accept this – because our bodies are the currency currently used by society to calculate our value. No wonder this question of how to be attractive is so integral to finding a partner. Your body/looks/outside appearance = your worth.

I know that we all want to be attractive – I include myself in this category. But I am positing that the restricted limitations to what we are told is attractive leave out the majority of the population. Which means most of us are left thinking that we are never enough. And whilst this might be great for the beauty industry, it's certainly not great for the self-esteem of billions of people worldwide.

I met a young woman at a dinner party recently. She was one of the most beautiful women I've ever seen. She was tall, slim, blonde and had naturally rosy cheeks. After a few glasses of wine, she admitted to me that she has always felt like the ugly duckling. EXCUSE ME?! (I tried not to blurt it out.) She explained that her sister is the good-looking one in the family – she's a model. Apparently, this woman has always been second fiddle in the looks department. Apparently, she has never felt 'enough'. This is when it was cemented in my mind: if someone like this, someone who has won the genetic lottery, still doesn't feel attractive, then this whole game is a farce. We can never win, even when we hold all the cards.

So, what to do? I'd like to invite you to do what I did. Create your own rules for the 'attractiveness game'. This means you stop living your life by the rigid rules of attractiveness that have been laid out for us and figure out what works for you as an individual.

Perhaps if you were to take a step back and observe, you would find that much of what you are currently doing is perfectly right for you. Hurrah! But that is the point. What is right *for you*.

And at the same time, we must stop judging others in this way. Comments such as, 'I don't see anyone here I like'; 'She could do with losing a bit of weight'; 'I like tall, dark and handsome'; 'He's just not my type'; 'A guy has to be taller than me'; 'She's a seven. You could do better' (all comments I have heard people make) just contribute to this game where we all end up as losers. It's hard to write this without sounding either patronizing or cheesy, but it's time to stop judging each other on our outside packages and initial impressions solely based on looks. This is something we have been further encouraged to do as a result of the onslaught of dating filters and image-based selections. At this current juncture in society, it seems that many of our digital interactions are designed in a way so that our only focus is judging people by these criteria. But I'd like to think that I have more to offer than my external package. What about you?

A particularly hideous trend is to label people's attractiveness on a scale: 'She's a nine'; 'He's a seven but thinks he's an eight . . .' I want you to do an experiment: close your eyes and think of the three people you love best in the world. What comes to mind when you think of them? Do you find yourself considering their perfectly symmetrical features or the silkiness of their hair? Probably not. Do you think of them as attractive? Probably yes, because you are thinking of them as the whole package of who they are, not as a collection of rateable features. Would rating any of them on a scale feel appropriate? Are they more than a number? Are *you* more than a number?

In our current climate, we tend to think that *being* attractive means *looking* attractive. But that isn't necessarily true. Attraction is a force that isn't singularly based on pure aesthetics: it's about a person's energy, charm, confidence, passion for life.

Let's say that you got a new haircut and you really liked it, so you were walking down the street on a sunny day, with a big smile and an extra spring in your step because you were feeling good about your hair. You happened to turn your smile on the lovely stranger waiting on the corner at the traffic lights. The stranger smiled back.

'Nice day, isn't it?' you say.

'It sure is,' they reply.

'I thought I'd treat myself to a coffee to enjoy in the sun.'

'Oh, I live around here. Where do you go for your coffee?'

And the two of you end up having a coffee together with a plan to meet up again. (True story, by the way.) Did this happen because your hair was so shiny and bouncy? No matter how brilliant the haircut, that doesn't seem likely. No, the powerful thing here was the confidence it gave you. You felt great. And this changed your behaviour, made you more open, and made others feel attractive in the process. This is the difference between *being* attractive and *looking* attractive.

And it starts from inside. What I see from working with people is that what they really want is to be able to show others who they are, their authentic selves. This desire is often couched in sentences such as 'I want to know how to make a good first impression' or 'I am shy. I want to be better at talking to people.' Feeling happy to show people 'the real you' is not only an integral part of self-development but it's also the way to become a more confident person. And once we step outside the confines of the attractiveness game, it's the real way to be attractive to others. Don't be afraid to show people who you are!

Sounds good, right? But how do you get there if you don't feel it right now? You do things that make you feel good. In fact, *only* do things that make you feel good. Stop forcing yourself to do the gruelling spin class if you don't like it and start up a weekly football game with your friends instead. Don't meet your negative friend for coffee; take a bubble bath. Skip the obligatory outing to the park with your old friends from school with whom you have nothing in common any more and treat yourself to an afternoon at the movies. My motto is simple: only do things that make you feel good, with people who make you feel good. This is an integral part of feeling attractive. Because if you feel attractive in yourself, you will be attractive to others.

Please, make whatever physical adjustments that you need to in order to make you feel better about yourself. A good haircut and clothes that suit your body type are good places to start. But don't be sucked into the narrow expectations of what it means to look attractive. Because *being attractive* and *looking attractive* are two separate things. One is how you feel in yourself – a vibe, which others can feel and makes them want to be around you – and the other is a one-dimensional projection to the world. Stop playing the game and start showing people who you are. You are enough.

3

Who Are You Going to Flirt with Today?

S O, WHO ARE you going to flirt with? We're talking flirting with intent here, flirting to get to know someone a hell of a lot better . . . As you know, my mantra is that you should approach every interaction the Flirtology way, but when it comes to serious flirting, if you're trying to find someone special, it helps to think about who you are looking for. Think back to Chapter 2, where you were considering your goals. Those goals are personal to you, and everyone's will be different. But if you did buy this book because you wanted to enter the dating pool in a serious way, then one important step on the way is to identify who your potential partners might be.

I was once talking to a man about his frustrations with his new girlfriend. From what he told me, they didn't seem like a good match. He worked in finance; she was an artist, surfing between friends' sofas. He was reliable and conscientious; she was a drifter, a dreamer. He liked to talk things out; she preferred to express herself in her work. He told me that he had just about decided to give up on the relationship. I said, trying not to be patronizing, 'Isn't it better to be by yourself than with the wrong person?'

'It's not that,' he said, 'it's just that, in the past, I feel like I haven't tried hard enough and just let the relationship slide. So, this time I wanted to make sure that I gave it my all.' Then it struck me: he was putting his effort into making it work with the wrong person.

So, how do you know if that person at the bar, or the first date sitting opposite you, might be right for you? If you are like a woman I once met, you will make him skip. Apparently, this is a good test of whether he's up for a laugh and doesn't mind making himself look ridiculous. Someone else told me that if a first date didn't share his food, that was a no-go. And for a second I thought perhaps these women were on to something. Who *wouldn't* want a partner with a sense of humour or who was generous? And wouldn't it be fantastic to devise a simple test that could check this out from the get-go? *'Skip!' I said.* But then I thought of my husband, who would flat out refuse to do the skipping test. And he hates sharing his food with me. (This is still contentious. I am not happy about it.) But if I had tried either of these 'tests' on him, I would have missed out on a wonderful partner. It's possible to be up for a laugh without responding to someone's every command, and sharing food isn't necessarily a measure of one's overall generosity. Although the refusal to do so might be an indicator of an only child.

One client told me that because she was assertive and confident, the man would have to be the one to approach her. Otherwise, she believed, she would be able to walk all over him. I understand why this woman would need someone equally confident, but just because someone doesn't step up to you doesn't mean that you can step all over him. Once again, the criteria she was using to gauge traits that she thought were important were completely ineffective. I can think of scores of men who are perfectly assertive but who might not necessarily hit on a complete stranger. These 'tests' get one thing right: they acknowledge that each of us is looking for particular attributes in a future partner. What they get wrong is that they are overly tricky and in the end don't really test for the qualities they are trying to uncover.

Not that I like to generalize about an entire gender, but I have had enough male clients to know that they often make the opposite mistake: they don't have enough criteria. For too many guys, when all of their friends are settling down and the pressure is on for them to do so too, they use two simple criteria to search out Ms Right:

1. She is pretty.

2. She is nice.

There, that's it. No skipping involved for the women. In fact, most of my male clients are very perplexed when I ask them what their five deal-breakers are in a partner. 'Oh, well, I've never thought of that before,' is the frequent response. This is not a better way.

Deal-breakers

So, what is a deal-breaker? A deal-breaker is an attribute that is, *for you*, crucial to find in a potential partner. It can appear as a personality trait, a type of behaviour, a fundamental belief or sometimes even a context (they must want to live in the city, or they must be up for spontaneous change, or they must be willing to travel). This isn't a wish list of nice-to-haves, like red hair or good abs, or a collection of vague adjectives like 'nice' or 'pleasant'. The deal-breakers are the *specific* attributes that really matter to you: the things that are going to form the bedrock of your compatibility.

Why are they important? The deal-breakers will play a major part in your future happiness with someone. They will help you to not be distracted by people who look shiny and fun, and focus instead on those who will make great long-term partners.

The other important point of deal-breakers is that they make it easier to move on when you meet someone who is nice but not the right person for you. They allow both of you to be released back into the dating pool to find better matches. I often hear women say that they went out with someone and he was great, but they didn't feel it was going to work. But they went out on a few more dates because he was nice and they didn't want to feel mean. Or they didn't go out with him again and then felt guilty. He was a good guy, after all; perhaps they were just being too picky? The deal-breakers alleviate this confusion. He or she could be the nicest person in the world, but if they don't match your deal-breakers, then they are not the right person for you.

The challenge: work out your deal-breakers – part one

First, get a piece of paper and make a list numbered 1 to 5.

1.

2.

3.

4.

5.

Write down the first five qualities that come into your head when you're asked to describe your ideal future partner. Don't think for too long at this point, just write the things that you think matter most. These can be traits, values, attributes or even contextual (job, where they live, etc.).

If you already had a list of what you were looking for in a partner, don't look at it. In fact, burn it. I guarantee it's doing more harm than good anyway.

Now, put this list to the side while you read the next section. We will return to it later.

Making a list of deal-breakers is a hugely useful tool, not just because it keeps you focused on those who will be a good match but because working the list out can teach you some valuable lessons about yourself. What is important to you? What do you value in life? What can you compromise on? To be effective, it has to be thorough, concise, specific and honest. I was once giving advice to someone who told me that he didn't think he had any deal-breakers; he just wanted to meet someone who was pretty and nice. But, after looking back at relationships in the past that hadn't worked, it turned out that there were a few things he thought were essential for a happy relationship. He appreciated someone who valued money in the same way he did, and someone who was happy to spend time with his very close-knit family. Even thinking about this had taught him some valuable lessons about what was actually important to him and where he might have been going wrong in previous relationships.

Another client was devastated in the wake of a split with his girlfriend, which in turn had followed the end of a previous relationship not long before. It was he who had done the breaking up both times. Why was he so upset? He felt he had invested huge amounts of emotion, time and energy, and he still cared for them both, so he was at a loss as to why the relationships had failed.

I wasn't that surprised when it turned out he had no idea what his deal-breakers were. Both women happened to be much younger than him, and in both cases he had started dating them because they were fun to be with and he was attracted to them. If he hadn't been looking for someone to settle down with, there wouldn't have been a problem. But at 42 he felt that he was at a different stage of his life. After we made a personalized list of his deal-breakers, he realized that in both cases the women were missing a few of his essential needs. In his case, it was wanting to live in the city and being intellectually curious. Neither of the women, nice as they were, met these criteria. For the long term, they were not a good fit. If he had known these deal-breakers before, it would have stopped him from getting so involved and affecting several people's hearts.

Deal-breakers – what might you look for?

Deal-breaker lists are incredibly personal and specific, and only you can know what yours might be. But here are some areas that I like to suggest that my clients consider.

Kindness. It's astonishing how seldom this one comes up. People almost never put it on their list, but if I suggest it to them, it always sparks a good response. I think to many people it's so fundamental it's not worth mentioning, but if it's what you're looking for, make sure it's on the list.

Similar interests. I hear this one a lot – people say they want someone who is into the same kinds of things as they are. If this is on your list, you might ask yourself why. Do you really want someone who is also into hip hop and seventies movies, or might it be fun to be with someone whose idea of a good time is something completely different? Exploring new horizons can be as important as shared activities, and it can be important in a relationship to have areas that are private to you.

Someone who is my equal. Again, this is something I often hear, particularly from successful women in high-flying jobs. If this is you, be honest: do you mean in terms of job, position, pay cheque? Again, think about why. It's fine to want someone on your intellectual level, but don't confuse this with their pay grade. Sometimes it works well not to have two enormously busy overachievers in one relationship.

Independence. Have an honest conversation with yourself about how you like to behave within a relationship: are you someone who prefers to have lots of 'me-time' or engage in lots of activities that are totally separate to the relationship, or do you like to entwine your lives? Either way is fine, but rough ground lies ahead if you try to combine the two approaches.

Geography. Long-distance relationships are tough. Be realistic about whether you think you can handle one. Similarly, if you're an urban dweller through and through, be honest about whether you want to live the rural dream.

Religion. For some people, religion doesn't matter much. For others, it's central to their lives. If religion is important to you, ask yourself the following question – will you be happy with someone who is happy for you to be religious but doesn't want to be involved, or is it important that they take part too?

And if you aren't religious at all, can you see yourself happily co-existing with someone who is? On both sides, never assume you will be able to change the other person's mind about something so deeply felt and personal.

Attitude to money. It's an awkward subject, and nobody ever wants to face it, but if you are a total spendthrift, it is going to be hard to get on with someone who likes to count every penny, and vice versa. There isn't a right way and a wrong way here, but it's worth ensuring that your values align on this one.

The goal is to meet someone who matches up with five out of the five of the deal-breakers on your list. If you meet someone who only meets four out of five, and you feel you could live without the missing one, then that is your choice. If someone has less than four, then this is not the right person for you in the long run.

Hang on, Jean, I hear you say, you have told us emphatically that we shouldn't be eliminating people from our flirting based on random criteria. You have been vociferous about the evils of dating-site filters and about seeing people as a collection of statistics. Aren't these deal-breakers just a variation on this theme – eliminating some of the world's population based on certain parameters?

Well, first of all, thank you for being so clever, but this is different. Why? Because these deal-breakers are not based on arbitrary statistics such as age, height, hair colour or preference for Thai food. This is a personalized list that is as much about you as it is about them; this is about working out *your own* core values and beliefs and making sure that your flirting life is not cutting across them. The aim is to protect yourself from trying to fit into a box that just won't accommodate who you are. So, of course you don't write someone off because you don't like his shoes or she has an extra-loud sneeze. Things like this aren't going to matter in twenty years' time. But what will matter? Someone's kindness, generosity, their sparkle, their fundamental self. Those attributes can't be measured in boxes, and they might not come wrapped in the package you were expecting.

So, some ground rules:

1. Physical attributes don't count. Tall, dark and handsome is essential for a leading man in a movie but not for your future life partner.

2. If you want to add 'Good sense of humour', change it to 'Shared sense of humour'. One person might find dark

humour amusing and another might be into puns, but both would say that they have a 'good sense of humour'. (Even though we all know that puns are not funny.)

3. You need to be honest. Don't adopt deal-breakers because you think they reflect well on you. A keen intellect is a fantastic thing, and many people would welcome it in a partner. But if what you really enjoy is spending time with someone who will laugh at your dumb jokes, just say so. Nobody is judging you for this list, so make sure that you aren't putting on a front.

4. Don't ignore what people tell you about themselves, hoping that you will be able to change or erode their beliefs with time. If somebody tells you that they don't believe in marriage or don't want kids, believe them. If on reflection you think this is something that matters hugely to you, then accept that your views on this fundamental issue don't align. Don't assume that they'll magically 'come around' through exposure to you.

5. Deal-breakers don't mean that the person's personality has to exactly match yours. If you are highly ambitious, it can be that another highly ambitious person would suit, but it's not automatic. Perhaps a more laid-back partner would counteract your tendency to be tightly wound, and help you kick back after a stressful period. The deal-breakers

aren't a list of your own best attributes, they are a list of what you value and what you care about.

6. Be realistic. It simply isn't likely that somebody is going to be both highly successful while not caring at all about material things, or that they are going to be incredibly family-orientated while simultaneously very independent-minded and spontaneous. If you are asking for a contradictory set of qualities, it probably means you haven't truly sorted out your own priorities yet.

7. Don't write a description of what you think your 'normal type' is. People are individuals, not types, and it may be that your 'type' isn't really working for you at the moment.

8. Sometimes the problem is that we don't know what we're looking for. Sometimes we think we do know what we are looking for but actually we want something completely different. For example, I had a client who said that she was looking for someone who shared her 'family values'. This sounds like it means someone who prioritizes family over other considerations and cares deeply about the family unit. But after probing a bit deeper, it turned out she actually meant that she was looking for someone who was self-motivated. There's nothing wrong with this at all, but it was a long way off from what she had thought was important. Incidentally, family values never made the list in the end but 'dog-lover' did.

The challenge: work out your deal-breakers – part two

Start a new deal-breakers list, numbered 1 to 5, just as you did the first time around, but this time keeping everything I've said in mind.

1.

2.

3.

4.

5.

First, is there anything you think you might have missed? Look at the box of potential deal-breakers on pp. 91–2. Does it give you any further inspiration?

Next, in light of everything I've said, look at each quality on your list and ask yourself *why* it seems important to you. Now, break it down to make sure that it's what you really mean. For instance, if you've written 'loves their job' on your list, consider why this matters. There could be many nuances to this seemingly simple deal-breaker.

- Is it because you love your job and are looking for someone who is equally passionate about theirs?
- Is it because your last partner continually moaned about their job and you don't want to go through that again?

- Or maybe it's because you are looking for someone who has the trait of passion?
- And if that's it, perhaps the real deal-breaker is that they are passionate about *something* but not necessarily about work.
- Because if they are hugely passionate about work, then there is a good chance that they will be spending much of their free time there.
- So, perhaps you are actually looking for someone who gives you a lot of free time to do your own thing?

You see how it helps to interrogate the real meaning behind each of the deal-breakers?

So, take your new list and go through each point. Ask yourself – is this what I really mean? Dig deep. If you've put 'fun-loving', what do you actually mean by this? Do you value devil-may-care spontaneity, a willingness to do the unexpected, or is it that you want someone who is good at enjoying the moment, while still remaining a responsible person? The two things are very different.

Do you have too many deal-breakers now? If you have more than five, it's becoming a checklist, not a thorough set of 'must haves'. Go through them again. To ensure that you have the right five deal-breakers, ask yourself if you met someone who had attributes 1, 2, 4 and 5 but not 3, would it matter in five years' time? If the answer is 'no', then it's not a deal-breaker. If it's 'yes', then it is.

And if you don't have enough? Think about it for a day or two and dig deeper. This list is about what is important to you. Other people will be a reflection of this. If you really can't come up with more than one or two, you are perhaps not examining yourself closely enough.

Just for fun, find your first list and compare the two. What has changed? What does this tell you?

Everyone's list is different. I should know, I have seen a lot of them! Your list is unique to you. Once you have the list, it saves you a lot of time. It keeps you focused on what you are looking for.

For example, let's say your list looks like this:

- lives in my city
- is sensible with money
- likes to be active and sporty
- doesn't want kids
- is reliable

Let's say you meet someone who seems great but lives in Paris and has no intention of moving. It means that no matter how witty they are, if you live in different cities (and are not prepared to move yourself), *you move on.*

Or you meet someone who is very interesting and attractive, sensible with money and seems reliable. But they definitely want kids and you don't. *You move on.*

Or this person constantly fails to turn up when you've arranged to meet them. Yes, they are charming and full of vim and vigour, and always very apologetic. But there doesn't seem to be any good reason for their extreme tardiness. And you know from your deal-breakers that reliability is crucial to you. *You move on.*

Or being active and sporty is important to you and it's how you spend most of your free time, but this person enjoys spending their weekends on the sofa reading and watching TV. *You move on.*

You might find this a bit strict. After all, there's nothing *wrong* with wanting to relax at weekends with a good book. And it doesn't mean someone is a terrible person just because they aren't always reliable. Maybe you should just cut them a bit more slack?

Look, you have carefully considered these deal-breakers. You haven't just pulled them out of a hat. This list is only five traits long and represents what is important to you. There are millions of people out there whom you could potentially match with. The purpose of this list is to help you streamline whom you should and shouldn't spend extra time getting to know for romantic purposes. It also helps you think about long-term compatibility instead of being distracted by the short-term sparkle.

Finally, I have a simple rule about deal-breakers. We all know that we don't always show our best selves when we're nervous, or stressed, or trying to make a good impression – all conditions that are common on a first date. And if we try to make someone tell us their deeply held principles and ambitions over the first cocktail, it can start to feel a bit like a job interview. So, I have a 'three-date rule' – if you think this person could have a minimum of four out of five of your deal-breakers, try to give them three chances. You might be surprised how they start to become physically attractive to you as well, once you start getting to know them. Take into consideration that some of the deal-breakers might be harder to uncover at first exposure. That guy who on the first date seemed uptight and no fun at all might have relaxed into his witty personality by date three.

I have had many a happy client email to tell me they are now in a wonderful partnership because of the deal-breakers: 'He wasn't my normal type, but he fit all the deal-breakers. And now we've been dating for five months. I think he's The One!'

Chemistry

Who would have thought that the most controversial thing I have ever said would have been whilst giving a lecture to middle-aged Brits in the basement of a bookshop in Bloomsbury? And what was this insidious proclamation that got the crowd so riled up? (I saw pitchforks being taken from underneath the seats.) I mentioned that one of the biggest mistakes people make when looking for a potential partner is assuming that there must be instant chemistry. Outrage ensued. 'Well, I might as well marry my brother if chemistry isn't important'; 'What is the difference between a friend and a romantic relationship then?'; 'What about sex? Do you not want us ever to have hot, passionate sex?' After I assured them that my deepest wish in the world was for them to have amazing sex, they calmed down a little.

But what was so challenging about this belief? It seems that we've all been conditioned to think that a future partner must immediately spark some primal urge in us, or that when we see a potential match, 'we'll just know'. There is a feeling that the spark must be immediate; it's not something that can happen later in the relationship, once the two people have gotten to know each other.

This idea that there must be instant sparks that come immediately or never at all, or that they are even a worthy indicator of whom you might do well with in the long term, is just a bunch of malarkey. I believe that is the scientific term for it. Don't get me wrong. If you are in an amorous mood and are looking for a friend for the night, if you *don't* have instant chemistry, then you've got nothin'. In short-term encounters, chemistry is imperative or don't bother. But if you are looking for something longer term, then the deal-breakers are essential for separating the shiny, sparkly things from the happily-ever-after partners.

How to find people attractive . . .

Having established your deal-breakers, what happens if you can't find anyone who seems to fulfil them? Sometimes, when people come to me worried that they have been single for a while, it turns out that the problem they have sounds rather counterintuitive. It's not that they don't know how to attract others; it's just that they simply aren't finding anyone out there whom they find attractive. It seems almost as though their flirting radar seizes up from lack of use. They feel as though they never meet people they fancy.

Not long ago, I was advising a young guy who even when he managed to go out with a girl, simply didn't know how to engage with her on a flirtatious level. He had been set up on a couple of blind dates, but the feedback from the women was that it was like going out with their younger brother. There was just no frisson at all.

When I fleshed this out a bit more with him, it seemed much of it had to do with how he regarded flirting itself. He told me that he hadn't been flirting with his dates for three reasons. Perhaps you can relate:

1. He didn't find any of them attractive.

2. He didn't want to lead them on.

3. He didn't know how.

We will take a detailed look at problem 3 in the next chapter. But what if you too can't find anyone you want to practise your moves on? Since this conversation with him, I have conducted an informal survey as to what stops people from flirting, and I found that not finding people attractive and not wanting to lead anyone on were as likely to stop people as the simple fact of not knowing how.

Let's start with the first point by talking about how to find people attractive. This is an area where we tend to assume our initial feelings are absolute. Yes ✔ No. ✔. And forever it will be. What we don't take into account is that finding others attractive includes many aspects other than immediate physical appearance. There's more to it than a quick glance in someone's direction, followed by our final assessment.

Whether we find people attractive, believe it or not, starts first and foremost with how we feel about *ourselves*: our mood, how we feel about our physical appearance (generally, but even more so in that particular moment), whether we are open or closed. We also don't realize that we can create favourable physiological responses through touching and laughing, thereby increasing how attractive we find others and vice versa. Both touch and laughter release feel-good chemicals in the brain, which creates more attraction. Definitely not something that can be produced with a quick eye sweep around a room.

So, let's imagine you're walking into a crowded party, hoping that tonight might be the night you find someone who really catches your eye. You look around . . . nope.

But think about your deal-breakers – physical attributes don't count, remember? You're looking for, say, someone kind, comfortable in their own skin, who has a healthy lifestyle, with whom you can have interesting discussions. How can you possibly know whether that person is here by casting your eyes around the room? What is the best way to find out whether people match that description? By talking to them, of course.

And luckily, armed as you are with Flirtology, this shouldn't be too hard. Flirtology is all about unlocking potential, both yours and other people's. This doesn't mean you should be 'settling' for someone you find physically unattractive, but it does mean that sometimes people's attractiveness reveals itself in conversation, not from a quick glance across a crowded bar. Maybe blonde women have never been your thing, but perhaps if you get talking to the one standing by the bar you'll find out that you share the same passion for synchronized swimming. And maybe you think you're not into guys with thinning hair, but once you're locked into conversation about your favourite episodes of *Sex and the City*, he suddenly starts looking much more Mr Big than Stanford Blatch.

. . . and how not to find them *too* attractive to talk to

Conversely, maybe you have no trouble flirting, until you meet someone who gets your heart a racin'. As we've seen with people who are naturally 'friendly' flirts, sometimes when they think the stakes are higher they lose their mojo. The minute they find themselves attracted to someone, the pressure builds, and all the fun leaks out from their conversation.

These two problems – not finding anyone attractive, and finding people too attractive to talk to – sound completely different. But, actually, the solution to both of them is the same. How can this be? Well, picture two scenarios that you might find recurring in your flirting life.

Scenario One: you walk into a room hopeful, excited that there might be some great flirting opportunities on offer. After a quick scan around the room you are deflated: once again, there seems to be no one here who might interest you. Why does this keep happening?

Scenario Two: you walk into a room hopeful, excited that there might be some great flirting opportunities on offer. And sure enough, right in your eye line stands the proverbial beautiful stranger. Wow. Just your type. But with this realization your brain freezes, your palms start sweating and you can't think of a thing to say. Why does this keep happening?

In both cases, you get stuck. And in both cases, the way to get past this block is, funnily enough, the same. What do you do?

You talk to people.

Why? Because knowing if you will find someone attractive involves more than just a quick sweep of your eyes. And it's just as foolhardy to think that you could 'like' someone with only a mere glance.

Give yourself the challenge of asking at least one question to five different people. And see how you feel about them after that. This way, the opportunity to be attracted to someone can involve more than their initial appearance, whether it means getting to know them on a deeper level or just making the encounter more pressure-free, because you are not trying to work up the nerve to speak with the unattainable 'One'.

Change the line at which you decide whether you 'like' some-one or not. Who knows, the foxy lady in the corner might become more Aunt Edna once you start talking to her. But the guy whom you wouldn't normally have looked twice at magically turns into George Clooney's single brother once you get the banter going. How could you possibly know after just a glance?

The aim is to reduce the pressure you attach to each single encounter and not miss out on potentially rewarding opportunities. Flirtology is all about pressure-free, easy connections.

If flirting is so easy and rewarding, then why don't we all do this more? One answer lies back in my conversation with my young friend and his second barrier to flirting: he didn't want to 'lead her on'. Too many of us are worried that somehow by engaging with someone you become responsible for them. While it's essential to be aware of others' feelings, and respectful of them, we are not in charge of them. Everyone is responsible for them-selves. And remember, too, the Flirtology way is not to steamroll in, pouting and pushing boundaries. The Flirtology way is no pressure. It starts with a simple question, which leads to the next, and the next . . . if it's not working, you disengage. Using this approach, it's not a question of 'leading people on', it's a question of seeing whether the two of you have anything to talk about. If not, no problem, you respectfully move on.

And I'm glad to say that in the case of my younger friend with the flirting issues, the story had a happy ending. After working out the problem together and recognizing what lay at the heart of it, he completely changed his behaviour. And, more importantly, he changed his attitude towards flirting. What had first seemed like something full of pressure and expectations has now become something that he actively enjoys doing. You wouldn't even recognize him. He is a flirting machine! He had it in him the whole time. Guess what? So do you.

4

Making Approaches

'WHY CAN I flirt when I'm not attracted to someone but can't when I am?' If you are mentally nodding your head right now, you are not alone. This is one of my most frequently asked questions. And it's where flirting moves from friendly openness into a more targeted activity. It involves a stepping up of gears, moving from the positive *attitude* of Flirtology into a state of *action:* flirting with intent. And, let's face it, while you might initially be a bit more nervous when confronted with a rollercoaster of pheromones caused by the Adonis at the bar, if you are using the tenets of Flirtology to guide you, this is where the real fun begins. Admittedly, flirting with someone you are attracted to can feel a bit nerve-wracking, but the other side of that coin is excitement! How much more thrilling is it to flirt with someone you really fancy? Personally, it's the one time that I can feel like the adrenaline-fuelled, fearless racing-car driver Mario Andretti, whilst still holding a drink.

The goal of Flirtology is to remove pressure from the flirting situation, leaving only fun. But there are always going to be those moments that feel a little more high octane: a party where you only know the host. A gallery opening where you are hoping to meet some works of art in human form as well. A work do where you know that the cute woman from finance will also be there. You wouldn't be human if you didn't feel a bit of a butterfly in your stomach about all the above. And that's what makes flirting with someone whom you are attracted to that much more exciting.

But while a couple of butterflies might add to the frisson, anything that feels like real pressure is the enemy of Flirtology. So, if you are feeling pressure, you do need to deal with it. Fortunately, you have a Flirtologist on hand to help.

Let's think of it in various stages:

Preparation

The first point about preparation is that you don't need to do anything extra. You are already doing it! Remember, if you are an averagely friendly person, and especially one who has taken the first chapters on board, then you should already be using every interaction you have as a reason to be friendly, approachable and open. Why should this be any different?

Let's think about the process of getting ready. For a start, **arm yourself in advance with a suitable mental model**. Too often, getting ready for an event, or anything that involves more than wandering down to the supermarket for a pint of milk, involves self-scrutiny and criticism: *'I probably won't find anyone to speak to'*; *'This dress doesn't do my hips any favours'*; *'Why am I always running late? I'm such a disorganized person'*. This is mental chatter; it tends to overwhelm us at moments of tension and can quickly turn into serious negativity. But are you going to be at your sparkling best in those moments when your internal monologue is giving you a serious talking to? No. So, turn it off.

In its place, remember the power of the mental model: **how we think affects how we behave, and this in turn affects the outcome**.

The thoughts going through your head as you walk through those doors will greatly influence your behaviour that night. Let's make sure they are thoughts that will help and not hinder. There are so many different ways you could perceive any situation, all of them equally valid, although it's the negative ones that we seem to cling on to. Why not make a conscious decision at the beginning of the night to choose the model that will help you to enjoy yourself and produce results, rather than letting your negative mind chatter influence which way the night will go?

Rather than *'I'm not going to know anyone at this event; it'll be really hard to find someone to talk to'*, change it to *'I'm sure there must be at least a few interesting people at this event; I am going to find them!'*

Rather than *'It's going to be difficult to get involved in conversations with strangers'*, change it to *'I like learning about others. Let's see who wants to share.'*

Yes, there may be moments when you find yourself wondering

who to talk to next, there may be people there who come across as a little unfriendly or moments where you feel uncomfortable. That's fine. Remember your mental model: *'Most people are friendly, just like I am.'* Move on and find one!

Many people find it useful to **set tasks** for the evening: *'I'll talk to at least six new people tonight'*; *'I'll make sure I approach at least three groups of strangers, if their body language looks open.'* The tasks should be within your own control. There's no point in setting the task of getting three people's numbers, as this relies on other people's reactions – on them being in the mood to share their number. This is something you simply can't predict. However, you could *ask* three people for their number. That *is* in your control.

Setting yourself tasks is a useful tool. It's a way for you to move the focus off you and on to the task at hand, which eliminates the personal, self-conscious element from the situation. Therefore, you are not starting an interaction because you think there is going to be some huge spark between you or because you think they're the best-looking person you've ever seen; you are approaching them because you have a task to carry out. This means you are approaching without pressure. If they turn out to be fantastic company, great. If not, just try someone else.

Just a couple of other tips for your preparation: if you're going out with a friend, **establish in advance what the night's going to be about**. If you're thinking of meeting new people while they're looking forward to a deep and meaningful catch-up, you're both likely to end up frustrated.

Finally, **be there early**. I am perpetually five (ish) minutes late to everything. Early birds amaze me. How do they do that? However, there are two instances in which I am capable of arriving early: an event where I won't know many people, and a massage. The massage is obvious. I can't fathom missing even a moment of bliss. But the event? This sounds counterintuitive; shouldn't you arrive when the whole place is buzzing and you can make an entrance? No. Arriving early gives you a chance to talk to the other early birds in a relaxed atmosphere. Is it easier to walk into a room of five people you don't know or 50, most of whom are already engaged in conversation? It puts you in control: as other people arrive, you have the chance to smile at them in welcome or to involve them in your conversation. By the time the room is heaving, you will have already struck up a network.

Entering

Right, so you're ready, you're feeling good, you've got your positive mental attitude going on; let's think about how you're actually going to enter the situation, the Flirtology way.

Remember, Flirtology is all about being efficient. Maximizing chances. If you are wondering why no one usually talks to you, could it be because your usual MO is to walk into a room with your head down, while making a beeline for your nearest life-raft (a friend, the bar) and then proceeding into a dark corner?

Look, that's not going to get you results. This is how we go about it the Flirtology way.

Look around. Keep your head up. Observe who is there. If anyone makes eye contact with you, acknowledge it. Smile, even.

By all means, do head for the bar. Hydration is healthy. However, head to the bar for the right reasons – not as a wet, slightly sticky safety net but as a goldmine of opportunities. You want to be in the high-traffic areas where it's easiest to strike up a conversation, and this is where the food and drinks are. But keep looking around you as you go. There is a phenomenon called the **mere exposure effect**, which I will explore later. Briefly, it tells us that people are more likely to have positive feelings towards those they have seen more than once, whose faces are familiar to them. So, make sure you are visible and that you are willing to make eye contact.

Look approachable

So, now that you have entered the room (suitable mental model in mind, head high, looking around), how should you project yourself? When you first see someone that you like, how will you attract them? It's not the shininess of your hair or your perfectly toned abs that will do it. The first and most effective way to attract people is to look approachable. How do we do this? Through body language. Fortunately, it's not a tricky code to crack.

The key is to make sure that your **body language is open**. What does this mean? Listen up, perpetual arm-crossers. It means looking up, looking out towards the room, head held high, arms *uncrossed* and shoulders open, turned towards the room. You might notice that this list does not include looking at your phone! The purpose of your phone is to watch funny cat videos when you are bored at work, *not* as a crutch when you are feeling nervous. Fiddling with it or pretending that you are having to check your massively important messages is fooling no one. And the act of looking downwards, intent on something else, signals your lack of interest in meeting anyone. You may think it is helping you not to look desperate, but in fact it only closes you off from opportunities.

A male client of mine was in London on business. He often ate dinner solo on these trips. He relayed the story of how the previous night, he and his phone went out to dinner. At a nearby table, there was a lovely woman who was also having dinner on her own. He admitted that he was so busy checking the screen that he didn't notice her surreptitious glances in his direction. It was only when he and his phone were sharing the last bites of dessert, and she gave him a big smile, that he realized what an opportunity had been lost due to his attention-seeking mobile.

Similarly, **do not sit down**. You may think that the security of finding a place to sit will make you feel more comfortable in this new situation, but resist the urge to take a seat. It makes you disappear. Literally, you become half the size. Sitting, you will be static, limiting your opportunities to encounter others. Your only hope for conversation is if someone sits down next to you. And let's hope that you like this proposed person, because you will be trapped with them. Exit strategies are much harder to implement sitting down. It's giving all the control over who you meet to other people. Think of it this way – close your eyes and imagine an encounter with an attractive stranger. Do it immediately. Now, recall the scene you have just conjured up: was that stranger standing at the centre of the room or sitting down in the corner near the loos?

While you're at it, think about *where* you are going to be standing. **You need to be at the centre of things.** Dark corners are conducive for creeping moss but not for finding potential love interests. Once you've been to the bar/snack table, move to the centre of the room. You need to maximize your chances of encountering people. You need to see and be seen. When you're standing in the centre of a room, not only can people spot you but it signals that you are available for conversation. We gravitate towards walls, corners and potted plants when we feel uncomfortable, because they offer us a false sense of safety. But we don't *need* a sense of safety because this isn't difficult, remember? It's a party, not a lion's den. Put your mental model to the test: '*I bet there are interesting people here.*' Well, what's the best way to find them? By getting out amongst them.

These are the body-language cues you should be projecting. But they are also the signals for which you should be looking. As you scan the room, keep your eyes open for people who are doing the same: those who have positioned themselves centrally, who are looking out and up, and who have open, approachable body language. And a smile always helps too.

Approaching

It's all very well standing there looking approachable and open, but we need to separate you from those smiley people in clothing catalogues. *You* are not one-dimensional. You can do more. Besides, if you just stand there, you are giving the control to everyone else. You need to be proactive, and the way to do this is to make the approach yourself. And, as we already know, this applies to all genders.

For many people, the million-dollar question is: how do you approach a perfect stranger? It's also where the hesitation begins. Let me guess: you think that everyone else is good at this, with one exception – you. Your mind goes blank, your palms start to sweat, you're convinced you won't know what to say and will end up blurting out the stupidest thing ever, the other person – and their friends – will laugh at you, and then a black hole will appear to swallow you up. Sound about right?

Part of the reason we think talking to strangers is so difficult is because we are attached to what their response might be. But we have already established that that is not our concern; it can't be. As I said back in Chapter 1, we are only responsible for our own part in any interaction. We have no control over other people's responses. I was out with my friends one night. My favourite hangout in London has bowling, karaoke, ping-pong and live music, all in one place. I had spent a great evening, chatting with the guys in the lane next to us during bowling. I played ping-pong with some others and danced the night away. Much fun was had. At the end of the night, I saw a guy standing there with two large glasses of beer. Full of good cheer from the night, I said to him with a smile, 'You must be thirsty!' He didn't say a word; he just looked right through me. Soon after, his girlfriend came over. He whispered something to her, and they both just looked at me. My brain took over, 'Well, they are obviously miserable people. I would hate to have their lives. They don't even know how to share a smile with a stranger. I feel so sorry for them.' It went on and on.

It threatened to ruin the whole feel of the night. And then I snapped out of it. I realized that it was not their job to make me feel good. Just as I had the right to say something to him, he had the right to respond however he liked. Whilst most people that evening were delighted to have some fun with me and my friends, engage in banter and flirting, no one that evening had the responsibility for making me feel good. However, most people that evening just happened to respond to me in the way that I would prefer.

This can be easy to lose sight of, but it is a crucial part of the Flirtology philosophy: **it's no one's job to make you feel good. That's your job.**

There is a second lesson here, one that is just as important: just as I was free to approach this person, he was free to respond as he'd like. **We all have the freedom to make our own choices.** This is crucial to Flirtology, because if I want to be able to try to engage people, I must recognize that they are also able to reject my advances.

And the third lesson stems from this freedom. **We should not be attached to other people's reactions.** When we are not invested in how others react to us, we do not need to censor ourselves. When we do what we really want to do, we are less attached to others' negative reaction. It's easier for us to think, 'Oh well, that's their prerogative', and their negative reaction has little impact on us.

So, it was because I felt free to make a comment to the man about the beer that in the end I couldn't take his reaction badly. If I want to empower myself to go up and engage someone, then I have to recognize that the other person is empowered to respond how they want.

So, all you have to do – all you *can* do – is make the approach. The other person can do whatever they want with this. They can give you a positive response, which is always preferable! They can give a short comment, or they can ignore you. Your task is not to get a conversation going. That is beyond your control. That takes two people. You only need to do your part. What happens after that is not just up to you but up to *the two of you*. A conversation will happen if the timing and the people at that moment are right.

Assuming you are following the simple and unbreakable rule that you are not harassing anyone or making anyone feel uncomfortable, most people will be happy to communicate with you. And even if it was you who made the approach, recognize that you are allowed to withdraw from it at any time. Just because you took the first step in an encounter doesn't mean you have to stay if you are feeling unhappy or uneasy.

Mostly, though, you will find that people are more receptive than you expect. As one of my clients relayed to me, after approaching strangers regularly for almost a year, 'You know, contrary to what I might have thought before I started doing this, 95 per cent of people are really happy to talk to me. I almost always get a smile back as well. Sure, 5 per cent of people aren't, but it doesn't matter. And because I do this so often, it's very easy for me to see that if they don't have a positive reaction, then it's due to them and not me.'

What do you do in the case of those 5 per cent? No, don't key their cars. If you can tell that they're not happy to be talking to you – and it will be obvious if you are paying attention – then no problem: you simply move on. (We will look at the tools to do this gracefully in the next chapter.)

How to approach

So, that's the theory about approaching people. How about the reality? What should you actually do?

First, **determine approachability**: take the lessons you have already learned about your own body language and apply them to others. To recap: are they looking up, looking around, are their shoulders open, arms uncrossed, are they smiling? If so, good: they are almost certainly a better bet than that person over there who is fiddling with their phone or whose head is bent deep in conversation with someone else. Now, look again . . . have they made **eye contact**?

Eye contact

My own research, backed up by other studies, has shown that the most powerful way to signal or receive interest is through eye contact. Those glances across the room at a stranger are some of the first ways we telegraph our interest to them. But how do you tell if this is friendliness, flirting or just your lines of vision getting tangled up together?

Without overanalyzing – does it really matter at this point? A glance is a glance.

If you really feel the need to assess the type of eye contact before you do anything, here are some basic guidelines:

1. **Frequency.** As a rule of thumb, one glance might be an accident, two might be coincidence, three or more is definitely a sign of interest.

2. **Length.** The length of time the eye contact is held is a definite indicator: long and lingering equals some form of attraction.

3. **Intensity.** You can tell if there is intent behind the eyes or if they are just looking in your general direction.

4. **Gesture.** If the eye contact is accompanied by a gesture such as straightening their clothes or unconsciously touching their face, then it is a signal of interest.

If it looks like a flirtatious move on their part, respond. How do you do this? Simple: you **smile**. Smiling is one of the key weapons in your arsenal. It not only gives a positive impression to others, but it also has a positive psychological effect on your well-being. It has been proven that the very act of smiling releases pleasure chemicals in the brain, feel-good enhancers. So, after smiling, if the other person is interested, they will respond in kind, and you can take it from there. You can't go wrong with giving an encouraging sign. Perhaps they didn't even realize they were interested until they saw you flash your pearly whites.

If no one has made eye contact, don't worry. It may simply be that they haven't seen you. You can still move on to the next step.

And that next step, obvious as it may seem, is to **move towards** your target. There's no point trying to signal your attractiveness and approachability from the other side of the room. You need to take some initiative. How close do you need to get? Close enough to be able to ask them a question but not close enough to be able to identify their brand of laundry detergent at this early stage. A few simple guidelines here: ensure that you are approaching them from the correct angle, which means definitely not from the back. You are trying to talk to them, not mug them. Walk around until you see an opening in the front – a position where their shoulders are facing towards you. Make sure there is enough space to speak: don't crowd them or squeeze in to the point where they feel uncomfortable. To create a potentially positive experience, the other person needs to feel comfortable from the outset.

All of this might sound like a rather complicated and lengthy set of instructions. In fact, the series of steps you take up to this point should be almost automatic: you enter, you look approachable, you observe the room, and you see someone you'd like to talk to. You move near them. Now, **just do it**. How many times have you wasted ages at a party deliberating about whether you should go up to that guy in the corner with the fantastic smile, only to find that just as you've found your courage, he's on his way out the door?

One of the reasons for our procrastination is that we over-analyze each encounter. Let's say you cast your eyes around the room and decide that you 'like' someone. Does approaching that person become easier or harder? I assume you feel more pressure once you've added the 'like' label, right? And if you *do* somehow manage to speak with this person, in this more highly pressurized atmosphere that you've unintentionally created, do you usually end up still liking them? Or, once they open their mouth, do they end up being cuter from afar and far from cute? Let's be generous and say that half the time you still find the person attractive upon speaking with them, but half the time you don't. For odds like this, why would you put yourself in a difficult position in the first place?

Remember your tools: you are exploring the scene with your new mental model of '*I bet there are some interesting people here.*' You had set yourself some tasks for the evening, including to talk to five new people. You can use this to remind yourself that this person is not an untouchable knockout; they are just part of your night's action plan.

As a rule, before you determine whether or not you 'like' someone, just wait until you've asked them one question. That's it. Approach them, ask a question, and then gauge their reaction. (In fact, don't just do this with one person, do it with everyone in the room.) But until then, keep it simple. Don't try to analyze everything first: is this the perfect person? The perfect opportunity? Will they give me the perfect response? In fact, don't think at all. Just go!

Asking a question

But what do you actually say? We can't have you charging up to someone and then doing an impression of an ice sculpture. You have to say something, right? If you are hoping to come up with that one line that will show this person how clever, witty and wonderful you are, don't. It's not possible. There is no such line.

But don't worry. Nobody ever embarked on a relationship because of the perfection of the first thing that somebody said to them. In fact, whenever I take my flirting tours out and about, I do an experiment: I ask the participants to approach each other and ask each other a question about something. This gets them practising but also demonstrates something we don't usually take into account: the true importance of having an amazing opening line. After they have spoken to each other for a few minutes, I ask the person who was approached to tell me what the other person's opening gambit was. Nine times out of ten, they can't even remember what was first said. So much for carefully crafted openers. The opening line is simply that: a device to open up the possibility of conversation. Or, as one NY female interviewee put it: 'You don't have to be dazzling in your opening line, then he has no pressure to respond in a witty way. Just be natural.' A good way to think about it.

With Flirtology, you don't need a 'line', you need an *attitude*: an attitude that says, 'I'm interested in talking to you and hearing what you have to say.' And the way to demonstrate this attitude is with an **open-ended question**.

The open-ended question is your primary weapon. By this, I mean a question to which the answer has to be more than a 'yes' or a 'no'.

On a recent flirting tour, one of the guys kept reporting back after his task, and he seemed a bit disheartened with the results. After going through his dialogue with the women, it went something like this.

Woman 1 at the gallery:

Him: 'That's an interesting painting.'

Her: 'Um, yes.'

Woman 2 on the street:

Him: 'Do you know where there's a fancy-dress shop around here? I am looking for a costume for my brother's party.'

Her: 'Um, no. Sorry.'

He was discouraged that the conversations weren't going anywhere and was assuming it was because of the women's attitude towards him as a person. He obviously wasn't their type. After hearing what had happened, I reassured him that he didn't need a personality transplant, he just needed to start with a better opener, one that would give the conversation half a chance of getting started.

What could he have done differently? For example, at the gallery, if he had said, 'That's an interesting painting. I like how the artist uses colours to convey the mood. What do you think?' He would have left some space for her to say something other than a perfunctory 'yes'. Or, in the case of the second interaction, asking for something obscure, like a place to buy costumes, wasn't likely to set someone up for success or make it easy to engage in a conversation.

On his next attempts, therefore, he made sure to ask open-ended questions and also questions which would fit the situation better. He not only had much better results but came to a simple but powerful realization: it wasn't his whole self he needed to change, just his opening gambit.

But if this all seems a bit too much to think about it, especially when confronted with someone whom you find attractive, then just use the magic question. It's incredibly simple and can be adapted to almost every situation. What is this magic question?

'What do you think of . . . ?'

For example, if you're at a bar, 'Have you tried this drink? What do you think of it?' If you're at an art gallery, or a bookshop, or live gig, then 'What do you think of this picture/book/band?' does the same job. Even if you're in a supermarket, the magic question can be adapted to groceries. 'What do you think of these avocados? Do you think these cute little things are possibly responsible for deforestation and supporting drug cartels?' You see, it's the perfect example of practised spontaneity. You have a general idea of what to ask in case the nerves kick in, but there's still room for it to be natural.

Let's break down why this is so effective:

1. You are acknowledging a shared experience (even if it's one as slight as standing next to them at the supermarket).

2. You are asking them something about themselves; this brings the opportunity of self-disclosure, an effective way to begin rapport-building.

3. You are making them feel important, by acknowledging that you're interested in their opinion.

4. You are giving them the freedom to give as much or as little of themselves as they want in their answer. There's no pressure; either of you can disengage as soon as you want to. Equally you can follow the conversation and see where it might lead.

The point is to start small, to get the ball rolling, to see where your one question might lead. One of my London research interviewees had an interesting analogy for the flirting experience and how it develops: 'It's like an arms race: starts small and with any luck it goes nuclear.' Yes, he was ex-military. How'd you guess?

Social contagion

This might sound like a dubious medical phenomenon. But this is something that you actually *want* to catch; it's a useful tool in your Flirtology armoury.

Why? Because if you are asking someone their opinion about something they have positive feelings towards, social contagion means you might get included in this love-fest.

It's not hard to imagine that if someone is speaking about a subject they love, they get excited. You are standing there. Why wouldn't you become enveloped in this cloud of excitement as well? Psychologists refer to this as social contagion: transferring emotions from one thing to another.

I first noticed this in practice whilst strolling around Selfridges in London with a male client. We were practising approaching women in the store and asking them their opinion about various items: bath gel, kitchen appliances, towels. It was only when we stumbled upon the chocolate aisle and started asking women about their favourite chocolate that their eyes lit up and they seemed to be in very good moods. They were dragging him around the chocolate section, pointing to all of their favourites. I noticed this same phenomenon on a flirting tour when a male member of the tour asked a woman in the pomegranate section how one was supposed to get the seeds out. It turned out her family had been growing pomegranate trees for years, and she was delighted to share her knowledge and stories with someone. Really, you have never seen someone so happy. Considering the mood of this happy individual, would this be a good opportunity to ask for her number? Yes. Yes, it would. You catch on quickly.

When people are in a good mood, they are much more open to you. This is probably not a breaking-news bulletin for you, but have you actually ever tried to utilize this little gem? To let it work in your favour? You can help enhance their mood by talking about things they like, doing activities they enjoy, or eating food they like with them. (Catch me whilst eating chocolate cake and I'll say yes to just about anything.) So, if you notice that someone's eyes light up when talking about a subject, take that as a green light to engage them on it.

Props

Besides the magic question, another way to think of what to say is to use **props**. No, you don't need to join your local community theatre for this one. Props are simply objects that help you think of something to say.

Picture the scene: you are sitting in your local coffee shop drinking your double cappuccino extra whip and you see some-one giving you numerous glances. You are pleasantly surprised to be receiving attention from this attractive stranger. But then your surprise turns into confusion, and then worry. What happens now? What are you supposed to say?

If I were to ask you to pull a question out of thin air, especially when you were already feeling a bit nervous, that would be hard, right? But what if I were to teach you the skill of how to anchor a question to a prop. The challenge isn't to think of a question but to recognize a suitable prop. From there, it would be easy to think of something to say in relation to the prop. So, in the coffee-shop situation, there are several examples of props.

The coffee shop itself: 'What do you think of this place?'

Or the food on offer: 'What kind of cake is that? Should I try one?'

Or the coffee itself: 'Is the coffee here nice?'; 'How do they make those intricate patterns on top of the lattes?'

There are props all around us. And some might be easier to spot than others. It's one of the reasons why it's so easy to speak to someone with a dog; dogs are the perfect prop and conversation-generating machines: 'What breed is it?'; 'What's its name?'; 'How long have you had it?' Though I did have one instance where when I asked my client what question he could ask someone about their dog, he came up with 'Does it bite?' Apparently, dogs aren't the best example of a prop for runners or people who deliver the post.

The beauty of props is threefold:

1. They make it easy to think of what to say at that moment, so they give you somewhere to start when you have to move quickly.

2. It's a more natural approach because it's taken from the context of what is happening at that moment. It's anchored in something the two of you are experiencing in the here and now. You are trying to avoid any clichéd pick-up scenarios, such as the time I was riding the escalator at the tube station and a guy said to me, 'Can I ask you a question about a business idea that I have?' I responded enthusiastically, entrepreneurial hat on firmly and ready to help. He presented his idea, and I began making suggestions. In the next moment, he started asking me about where I was from . . . and then for my number. I wasn't happy when I realized that I had been duped and that I wouldn't be contributing to any new business empires that day. This illustrates why a shared moment is a much better conversation starter than a pre-prepared gambit.

3. You are asking people about their opinions and preferences, which often leads to self-disclosure. You can build rapport much more quickly when people reveal things about themselves, and this could potentially lead to a more interesting conversation than simply talking about the weather. As one of my clients says, 'I don't like small talk, but I like prop talk.'

There. That was easy. So easy, in fact, that it feels almost too obvious. All I have told you to do is to enter a room with confidence, approach a stranger with a question, and listen to their response. Sitting in your comfortable chair, reading these words, it doesn't seem so hard. Now, we just have to move from the theory to the actuality. And it gets even easier with practice. The first step is just this: practise, practise, practise. Just start asking people questions, wherever you are.

♡ The challenge: try to build a rapport with someone

In Chapter 1, I asked you to go and ask strangers for information. It wasn't that hard, was it? Now, I want you to build on what you have already done by trying to elicit from them more than a simple fact. I want you to try to create a connection with someone.

The task: once a day, for the next week, try to build rapport with a stranger. You can do this by asking questions that allow them to share their preferences with you and then building on that question by using:

1. **Commonality** – 'Oh, I like that too' or 'I thought I was the only one who didn't like that place.'

2. **Self-disclosure** – sharing something personal about yourself and having them do the same. 'Is it far to walk? I shut down after one mile.' Or 'What would you recommend drinking at that place? Any favourites?'

Rapport is established when the person involved shares something with you that goes beyond simple information. It's about them disclosing in a small way their likes or dislikes, something about themselves. It doesn't have to be a huge life-changing revelation – we are just looking for that extra human connection.

The guidelines:

1. You must make it clear that you are specifically asking the question to them. Don't think that if you only ask 'halfway', that you halve your chances of being rejected!

2. You can still start with something simple, like asking directions. But the goal is to work towards asking people their preferences, such as, 'Do you know of any good coffee shops around here? Which is your favourite?' This will give the best opportunity for someone to self-disclose and share something about themselves.

3. Ask an open-ended question, which leaves room for the possibility of a small conversation, should you both be in the mood.

4. Have no attachment to their part in the interaction. Your task is for you to ask someone a question. The success or failure of you completing your task is not tied to their response. Again, success is only tied to whether you try.

Examples:

- In the coffee shop: 'Which pastry would you recommend?'
- On the street: 'Are there any good pubs around here?'
- At the supermarket: 'Have you tried this before?'

Barriers

Making the approach is something that my clients often think of as the hardest stumbling block in the whole of Flirtology. In their heads, they can imagine themselves keeping a conversational ball rolling once they're in the midst of it. They have, after all, been in lots of conversations with people, so the assurance is based on past experience. But how often have they had the experience of approaching? It's no surprise then that the thought of that very first move often scares them. As more than one client has put it: 'I'm fine once I'm in it. It's the first part that is the hard bit.' When they rationalize in their heads as to why this is so, they find the following reasons:

'I don't want to be seen as creepy'

I have never heard a woman phrase it like this, but it's a common statement from men. They don't want to feel like some kind of sleazeball, interrupting a woman's night out with their unwanted approaches. Who wants to be *that* guy? Well, that's a very laudable attitude. And, indeed, if your preferred method of approach was to go up to a perfect stranger and do your best impression of an octopus, then perhaps you might have a point. But you're not creepy. And if you're going about it the Flirtology way, you're not going to come across as creepy. Just remember the advice: ask a question and then assess. The key moment here is the assessment, because in that space between your approach, your first question, and her reaction, you can see how your approach was perceived.

Creeps just barrel on through it, either not caring or not being aware enough to see whether their approach is welcome.

And this is the key: if that reaction is not positive, then you will move on. What is so creepy about having asked a question? And if the reaction is positive, then no sleaziness is involved. Fear of being seen as creepy has robbed many men of great opportunities: don't be one of them.

'Maybe he won't like it'

This is the female equivalent of the male 'creepiness' line – the notion that men will somehow take it amiss if a woman goes up to them. We've already covered whether women should make the approach in Chapter 1, and you'll remember that there's absolutely no reason why not. In fact, most men positively welcome it.

And ask yourself this: if you're a woman, do you like it every single time a guy approaches you? Probably not. Sometimes you do, sometimes you don't, depending on the guy and how he does it. So, what makes you think that guys wouldn't feel the same way? There isn't one blanket response here, but the test and assess method is equally applicable to everyone. Besides, if you are an assertive woman in every other area of your life, would it even be a good match if you approached a guy and he didn't like the fact that a woman had taken the initiative? Think of it as a good weeding-out mechanism!

'I will lower my value by taking the initiative'

This is a slightly darker variation of the female excuse above: the notion that somehow by relaxing her ice-goddess pose and deigning to talk to a mere mortal, a woman is somehow making it too easy for the man in a way that will rebound on her reputation. I am still not sure how a woman taking the initiative can negatively impact her value; I would assume it would only add to it. But this is a story that has been passed down through generations in many cultures. Its effect means women remain passive, stagnant, waiting. They have no say in whom they get to talk to. If you find yourself thinking like this, try to get to the bottom of what exactly has led to this thought. And do you really feel that the type of guy you want to be with is going to be thinking about your value in this way?

'They will laugh at me'

This is a universal fear: both men and women find their minds spinning ahead, picturing the moment when the person they approach humiliates them with their public and unkind refusal. Without getting into the ins and outs of how likely this is to happen (not very), think about what your mind is doing to you here: it has made up a story in which it is always assumed that you will have a negative experience. But that is all it is: a story, manufactured out of some worst-case-scenario imaginings.

The best way to counter this fear is to meet it head-on. Get enough practical experiences of approaching in your repertoire and I promise you will be pleasantly surprised at how most people have positive reactions. The trick is to increase your sample size, so the next time your brain starts telling you that you will be laughed at, the cells in your body can counter with all of the positive experiences you have racked up.

'That person is too good-looking for me; they're out of my league'

Another universal fear. But we have already discussed the attractiveness game and the difference between someone being an attractive person and looking attractive at first glance. Besides, people are not pegs on a rating board, allowed only to talk to those in their attractiveness bracket. If they were, the beautiful people would have a dreadfully boring time, never able to speak to the rest of us. People have lots of assumptions about 'good-looking' people. I have known a few, and I am happy to report that they are just people too. In fact, many of them would have no idea that they are part of the beautiful crowd. Attraction is a subjective thing. Don't write people off because of how you imagine they perceive themselves. Talk to them and see what they are really like instead.

'I'll get myself into a situation that I can't get out of'

Look, as much as Flirtology is about sunshine, smiles and puppy dogs, it's also about not being a dimwit. I know that you are aware of common-sense principles: don't approach people in dark alleys, don't speak to people if you are by yourself at night or any other time you feel uncomfortable. If someone is looking at you weirdly or giving off bad vibes, avoid them. Trust your instincts.

However, under 'regular working conditions', you should always be able to get out of situations. Why? Because you don't owe anyone anything. Sorry if I sound repetitive, but it bears repeating: assuming you are following the guidelines of being a good human, you are only responsible for yourself, not other people. So, if you make an approach, ask someone a question and then don't have a good feeling about them or their response, there is no reason why you have to stay a second longer. Unless you are stuck in cement, you can always leave. In fact, in extreme cases, you might not have to say anything else at all, just turn around and go. In less extreme cases, just say something vague like, 'OK, thanks' and then just turn around and go. Check out the **graceful exits** in Chapter 5 if you want to learn more about how to do this.

Soon, you will start to see that approaching people and starting up conversations isn't the root canal that you'd envisaged. Great! But then what? How do you take a conversation at the supermarket about the merits of almond milk and turn it into a full-on flirtatious encounter? Or, indeed, how do you bow out gracefully? Turn the page and all will be revealed . . .

5

Moving It On

Ionce instructed a flirting tour-goer to go up to a woman in a supermarket. Because I knew that he had a penchant for pecorino, it made sense for him to ask the woman standing next to the cheese counter a question on the subject. He asked for her opinion; she gave it to him with a smile. She then asked him which cheese he preferred . . . and he walked away. When I asked him what on earth he was doing, he said, 'But, Jean! You programmed me to ask the question, you didn't program me for what to do next!' Of course I didn't. The point of an open-ended question is that we don't know where it is going. But that is also the joy of it. It could lead us anywhere . . .

But not knowing how to respond when someone bats a question back at you is not uncommon. I've seen it happen on my flirting tour, particularly with the men. Quite often they will start a conversation, receive an encouraging opening, and then just walk away from the situation. My theory is that this comes from a 'quit while you're ahead' mentality. They're so pleased that they weren't initially rebuffed that they don't want to risk continuing the encounter with the possibility of getting rejected later.

For some people, moving things on to the next level can seem like the scary bit. But while I can't give you a point-by-point breakdown of every possible conversation in existence, that doesn't mean that I can't help guide you into the next stages of the encounter.

What do I mean by moving things on? Well, a flirting encounter can go several ways:

1. **Friendly or flirting?** They respond to you, but you can't read their response. Are they interested or not? And how should you play it?

2. **The knock-back.** They respond negatively, rebuffing your advances. This feels like the worst possible outcome: you tried, you did your best, you got rejected. Before you start feeling sorry for yourself, this is the exact moment where your Flirtology training on rejection should kick in.

3. **The graceful exit.** They respond positively, but you decide you're not interested. The fear of being trapped with no way out is enough to stop many people from making the approach in the first place. How do you disentangle yourself from an encounter if it's not working out for you?

4. **The green light.** They respond positively, looking interested. Wonderful. Isn't this what we were hoping would

happen? Then why do you feel so much apprehension? What if you screw this up?

Never fear. I am here to guide you through all the possible outcomes. And it starts by recognizing that all these potential problems are future worries – to be dealt with in the future, if ever at all. At that moment when you step up to someone, none of these things have happened yet. Don't let yourself be constrained by a plethora of outcomes that only exist in your imagination.

1. Friendly or flirting?

This is the number one question I get asked about this stage of the game. 'How can I tell if this person is flirting or just being friendly?' It's part of the initial step of any encounter: determining whether they are interested in you. (And, just as importantly, whether *you* are interested in *them* – sometimes we can get so carried away by making sure we are being as alluring as possible that we forget to consider if we actually like this person.)

To determine interest, all you have to do is listen to them. And respond. Sounds easy, right? In theory, yes. In practice, much harder. Why? Because in order to listen and respond, you must be in the present moment. This is a place where we reside infrequently. Especially when we are nervous, self-conscious and standing in front of someone whose genes we admire. Listening, active listening, means not only actually 'listening' but also showing that you're listening. Looking someone in the eye, nodding, reacting and responding to what they are saying with your facial expressions are all part of this moment together.

In anthropology, we have a tool called **participant observation**. Traditionally, anthropologists use it as a way to be involved in a culture but not so immersed that they can't make observations as to what is going on. It helps them to stay one step removed and, therefore, able to see things more clearly.

What does it mean for our purposes? Well, when people are in conversation, particularly with someone whom they find attractive, it's easy to feel self-conscious. But the word *self*-conscious is our first clue about what is going wrong. Focusing too much attention on ourselves, worrying about what we are saying, how we look, what the other person must be thinking about us, is a reason why things start to unravel.

There is only so much energy available in any given interaction. Do you want to spend that energy on yourself, being conscious of yourself, or do you want to spend it on the other person? Participant observation is a way of helping you shift the focus. Did he just blush at your cheeky comment? Did she just absent-mindedly begin stroking her arm when you mentioned your fondness for fluffy kittens? When you are not focused on yourself, you can see the effect you are having on others. This is when the fun of flirting begins!

I often use this tool when I am out on the streets with clients, helping them practise approaching people. After their interaction with a stranger, we regroup. The first thing I ask them is, what did you observe? Usually, during the first few interactions they haven't noticed much, because they are still focusing on themselves. By the third interaction, it starts to become fun. They can begin to describe the other people in the interactions in much better detail. Because they aren't so focused on themselves, it helps to alleviate their feelings of awkwardness. People are interesting. The distinguished English gentleman in the three-piece suit admits, sheepishly, that he loves hot chocolate. 'My wife thinks that I drink too much of it,' he divulges. The glamorous woman with the five bags of shopping and mile-high heels recommends that we take a cab when we ask for directions: 'It's much too far to walk.' The ex-military guy gives us precise directions and then eyes up my client when he sees her an hour later, as if to say, 'Why aren't you currently at the destination that you asked directions for, soldier? Drop and give me 20!' It's amazing what you can learn about someone in a short amount of time when you use participant observation.

Task: improve your observation skills

In the last chapter, I asked you to go up to a stranger and try to make a brief connection with them. Now, I want you to think about those people. What can you remember about them? If you've done this exercise recently, you can probably remember their approximate age, height, gender. Anything else? Clothes, hair, distinguishing features? Could you describe them?

It's quite likely you can't, because if you were new to doing this you were probably more focused on what you were saying, your level of nervousness and whether you had butterflies. In other words, you can remember yourself in that moment but not the other person.

So, I want you to try it again. This time, I want you to do the exact same exercise: go up to someone in the street and ask them an open-ended question: 'Can you recommend a good cafe around here?'; 'Do you know how to get to the nearest tube station?' While you're doing it, I want you to notice two particular things about their appearance. Maybe the colour of their hair or what kind of shoes they had on.

And when that's finished, I want you to do it again. But this time, instead of being focused on a physical characteristic of that person, I want you to try to understand something about their demeanour in your interaction together. Does their body language look open or closed? Do they lean in to the question or seem to back away? What can you tell about their reactions simply by observing? Do they seem easy-going, stressed, in a hurry, up for a laugh? Can you tell anything about their personality?

And now, think about whether, by taking notice of the other person like this, you have been quite as conscious of your own nervousness in that moment. Did the encounter feel more fun to you, or less? Do you feel you made more of a connection?

Two things happen when you shift your attention from *you* to *them*:

1. You don't have the space to think about yourself. Your attention is on them.

2. They like it! Who wouldn't like the feeling of someone genuinely listening and paying attention to them?

*

This is what I would like you to try in your next encounter. Make sure you are participating fully in the conversation but are not so immersed that you can't observe your behaviour and the behaviour of the other person. This means that if suddenly they take a step back and fold their arms, you can pick up on this and consider if perhaps you have just unintentionally said something that put them off. Or if you say something cheeky, you can observe how they take it: do they become nervous? Do they laugh? Do they bat the same feeling back to you? And when you are paying attention to them like this, do you find that it increases or lessens your own nerves? Do you enjoy the flirting encounter more?

The point at which the flirt takes on a life of its own is when you stop reminding yourself to stay in the moment and instead just enjoy the ride.

Being in the moment

One very important point about participant observation is that you must be *in the moment* in order for this to work. In other words, you are not fretting about what you have just done or worrying about what your next step should be. How can you observe your interaction if you are operating in the future tense or stuck in the past?

Some tools to help you do this are:

1. Connect with your breath.

2. Make a gesture to remind you to be in the moment. My friend likes to make a quiet click with her fingers, by her side, to remind her to snap out of it when her mind races ahead.

3. Now you have centred yourself, switch your focus back to the other person. Notice one new thing about their physical appearance. Now, pay attention to their body language, what they are saying and how they are saying it.

H.O.T. A.P.E.

In my research across four different cities – New York, London, Paris and Stockholm – most respondents said that it could be hard to tell the difference between friendliness and flirtation. The exception was Paris, where one Parisian male explained, 'If a man sees a beautiful woman, he is never going to be friendly. He will always be flirting.' In cultures which were more into subtle nuances, there was more uncertainty about whether people were friendly or flirting. In London and Stockholm, for instance, almost all of the males in particular found it hard to tell at times. 'Women shouldn't be so coy, and men shouldn't be so insensitive' was the suggestion of one helpful London male. Out of all the flirting research I undertook, my favourite discovery was the 'fact', repeated by a large proportion of the London males, that you could tell a woman was flirting with you because she would touch her hair. The only problem was that it was completely imagined. No London female ever reported doing this, at least not on purpose with the intention to flirt.

So, it's not surprising that both men and women get very nervous that they will read the signs wrong. And, equally, being aware of the signals that you are giving out can ensure that you are sending your intended message. Half-heartedness or holding your cards close to your chest is the enemy of successful flirtation!

From my cross-cultural research into flirting, I have discovered there are six ways in which people can understand when someone is flirting with them. These six ways are also how people convey their interest to others. I have created the acronym H.O.T. A.P.E. as a breakdown of the flirting signs.

If you want to work out if someone is friendly or flirting, then this is the handy checklist you need:

- Humour
- Open Body Language
- Touch
- Attention
- Proximity
- Eye contact

Let's break them down.

H – Humour. The benefits of humour work in a few ways. As we've already seen, everyone says that they are looking for someone with a 'good sense of humour'. And we've established that what we really mean is someone who shares our sense of humour, someone we can laugh with. Humour is a great weeding-out mechanism to see who is a good match. Sure, they might have great hair and share your passion for ping-pong, but if you have to say 'Only joking' after each wry comment you make, can you imagine doing that for the next twenty years? However, if someone is making an effort to throw their best lines at you, and you readily accept and bat them right back, then it's a very good sign. Or, you could be like the London males and know that she likes you if 'she laughs at my crap jokes'.

So, is this person trying to target you with their jokes, trying to create a shared space between you (as opposed to telling funny anecdotes to the room at large)? If so, it's a very good sign.

O – Open Body Language. Stop for a moment and sneak a peek. What is the body language telling you about the person with whom you're speaking? Positive signals are if they are squared up, facing you, with their feet pointed in your direction. Why the feet? It's a useful tip: if they are angled towards you, it shows the person is into your conversation. If they are angled away, simulating someone ready for a quick exit, then they are probably planning their getaway. Similarly, if their arms are folded across their chest or shoulders turned slightly away from you, they are not really into it.

T – Touch. This is the big one. 'It's what makes you culpable. Once you touch, you are flirting. There is no deniability,' as one friend put it. Yes, some of you might be naturally touchy-feely people, but if someone touches you, there is a high chance that they are flirting. Touch also releases oxytocin, the hormone we are flooded with when we are happy. In one experiment, couples who engaged in a warm touch exercise, during which they touched each other's neck, shoulders and hands, had more oxytocin in their saliva than couples who did not engage in this exercise. This means that people who touched each other had more of the feel-good hormone rushing around their systems. So, if someone is reaching out to you, it's a pretty good indicator that they want more than just a friendly chat. Whether this is something you welcome will depend a lot on whether they know how to use this tool appropriately. And how cute you find them!

A – Attention. This one might seem like an obvious one. If the person is paying more attention to you than everyone else, it's a very good sign. As one London female interviewee said, 'You know he is flirting if he is telling a story to the whole group but tells it more to you than anyone else.' Or as a London male put it, you know you are interested in someone 'when you are at a dinner party and know you should be paying equal attention to the people on both sides of you, but you really only want to speak to one of them'.

Many admitted it was much easier to observe this happening for other people than notice it for themselves. Once you are in that moment, it's hard to keep perspective, and this is another great example of why participant observation is a useful tool. But if you suddenly find that it feels like the two of you are in a dreamy haze and the rest of the world has temporarily melted away, then you know there is mutual attention happening.

P – Proximity. This has two different aspects. If when you first spot someone they're way over on the other side of the room, and then, suddenly, you find them much closer to you, they have probably moved location for a good reason . . . You! They could well be getting ready to flirt.

But you can also tell if someone is flirting by the space they take up as they talk to you. If they are standing slightly closer than normal, then it can be a sign. It's about creating a more intimate space by leaning in to speak softly, making it easier for your arms to gently brush each other. Other benefits of standing close to someone means that you can smell each other. This smelling of others is probably happening without you even being aware of it, unless the other person is wearing strong perfume, or has had some seriously good hummus for lunch (read: lots of garlic). Pheromones have become a talking point of late, but there is actually some scientific analysis to back it up. Using brain imaging, Swedish researchers have found new evidence that women and men can in fact send and receive subconscious odour signals. The scientists, led by Dr Ivanka Savic of the Karolinska Institute, found that the hormone-like smells 'turn on' the brain's hypothalamus, which is normally not activated by regular odours.

That sweet, sweet fragrance? Well, that's you and the smell of successful flirting.

E – Eye contact. In my research, this was the most often talked-about and most powerful way that people could sense when someone was flirting. Phrases like 'meaningful gaze' or 'lingering glances' were often mentioned. So powerful was eye contact that one woman suggested avoiding it altogether: 'You can't make eye contact with a man in Paris, or he will Lock You Down with his eyes.' We've already seen how eye contact across a room can signal the start of a flirtatious encounter. But how much a person makes eye contact during a conversation is also an indication of their interest. If they are scanning the room over your shoulder, then it's unlikely they are focusing their flirtatious energy on you. But if they are focusing their gaze on yours, signalling a spark and repeatedly catching your eye, then it's fair to say you have their attention.

What do you do when all the H.O.T. A.P.E. signs are there? One of the New York interviewees put it perfectly: 'You just keep upping the ante. You look and they look. They move closer and you move closer. They touch your shoulder, you touch their hand. They say something cute, you laugh . . .' We get the picture.

False starts

What if you're having a great conversation that suddenly seems to fizzle out? One minute the banter is flying, and the next, everything suddenly grinds to a halt, topic exhausted and both sets of eyes casting around the room for the next thing to say. If this happens, relax. Return to basics: ask them a question and see what happens. What question? The question that everyone knows the answer to: ask them something about themselves. One suggestion is, 'What do you do for fun?' Remember what we said about social contagion? Become part of their good mood as they wax lyrical about their rewarding work at the dog rescue centre. Pretty soon, they'll be wanting to trim your nails and wash your coat till it shines as well!

Be careful not to make the mistake of doing absolutely anything to avoid a gap in conversation. This usually means you are taking up most of the conversation space and not letting the other person get in a word edgeways for fear of the dreaded awkward silence. The odd stutter in conversation is natural if you're talking to someone you don't know. Don't be afraid of the occasional pauses; they leave space for the other person to ask a question or steer the conversation. However, if you are having to pick up most of the slack, think about whether you're having to do too much to make the conversation flow. It could mean that the conversation has run its natural course and it's time to move on.

How do I know if they're single?

It's something we'd all rather avoid: batting your eyes, smiling seductively and throwing out your best one-liners, only to discover after your interest has been thoroughly piqued that they are in a relationship. It's even worse if they are trying to pull a fast one by purposely avoiding the issue.

My recipe to avoid this situation is to ask the following question: 'What did you get up to last weekend?' It's a good question anyway, allowing someone the opportunity to talk about what they feel interested in.

But making it specific – what did they do *last* weekend – means that because the events have happened in the past, it's much harder to make things up on the spot.

Also, you can tell by the language – 'we' – or the activities – 'went to my child's piano recital' vs 'joined my friends at a bar' – whether this person is single or partnered. You will, in a casual way, bring to the surface any hidden partners.

2. The knock-back

For many people, their greatest fear is that they put themselves out there and get rejected. But take a deep breath and think it through. Does this have to be such a bad thing?

In Chapter 1, we've already talked about rejection and why it isn't something to fear. Let's remind ourselves of the multiple reasons why:

- It's a good weeding-out process and helps eliminate people who aren't right for you. You don't want to be wasting your time on someone who isn't a good fit.
- It's not a judgement on your whole personality. When it comes to approaching strangers, you don't know them and they don't know you – the only interaction with this person so far is a question or a brief conversation.
- There should be a direct correlation between your level of hurt and the amount of time you've invested. Rejection might hurt if it comes after a six-month relationship, but after a two-minute conversation? Where your investment is almost nil?

- You are not a failure just because this person isn't a good match. How could they all be?

But what if I were to tell you that rejection can also be empowering? I was the wing-woman for a woman in her thirties who had always found it difficult to step out of her comfort zone and approach people. I'd schooled her thoroughly in the principles of Flirtology: that it is perfectly acceptable for women to make the first approach; that when you look at it from the Flirtology point of view, there is no pressure; that all she had to do was ask one question and assess. We entered the bar together, and she saw someone she liked the look of. I sent her off to make the approach. She returned a mere moment later, and I could only assume that things hadn't gone well. Surprisingly, she was bursting with enthusiasm, but not because he had been interested. He wasn't, but his response appeared to be irrelevant. What was most exciting to her were her own actions. She had been brave enough to make the approach, and when knocked back, guess what? She found that it didn't actually hurt her feelings. The pain of what she had built up in her head was revealed to be nothing much after all.

This was a crystallization of two points that I have seen repeatedly with my Flirtology clients:

1. The abstract *fear* of being rebuffed is much stronger than the *reality* of it.

2. The feelings of empowerment and freedom that come from doing what we want to do override everything else.

*

And the next time this woman sees a mysterious stranger in a bar, she is going to feel a great deal braver about going over to say hello. She knows a powerful secret: rejection doesn't have to hurt, therefore she has nothing to lose. Knock-backs happen. It's how you handle them that matters.

3. The graceful exit

But what if it's the other way around? What if it is you who wants to disengage? You saw that woman across the room, you smiled, you approached and you asked her your question. Now she's enthusiastically chatting away about everything under the sun, but you've realized that, as nice as she seems, you are now done. Problem is, she is just getting started. You certainly don't want to be unkind, but nor do you want to get locked into a whole evening with this person or, worse, a date, just out of politeness.

A woman I knew had been looking forward to her office work party; she saw it as a prime flirting opportunity. Sitting on the sofa with a divorced colleague, she was ready for the chance to flirt. Problem was, he'd taken it as a chance to get out his phone and show her every single snap of his kids. Five minutes into the conversation, she had figured out that she wasn't interested in him or the four hundred photos of his daughter's ballet recital. Why couldn't she escape?

I once introduced two friends to each other at a party and was happy to see them still chatting away nearly an hour later. When I finally cornered my friend and excitedly asked her what she thought of Tim, she replied, 'Oh, he's all right, but not really my type.' So, how come she had spent so long in the kitchen wrapped up in conversation with him? 'I didn't want to be rude,' she said.

What is happening here is that people are becoming trapped by what they perceive as their own niceness. I say 'perceive' as niceness, because if you consider the situation in a different light, then perhaps keeping things going beyond their natural end isn't the kindest thing to do. People are allowing various emotional preconceptions to get in the way of what they should be doing. Let's look at it in detail.

First, and it's worth repeating this to yourself, **you are not responsible for the other person's emotional well-being**. In any encounter, yes, you do have a responsibility as a human: to be considerate of the other person and not to be gratuitously rude or unkind. But just having a brief conversation with someone does not make you the guardian of their feelings. If we all took owner-ship of ourselves, we wouldn't be so tied into others in this way.

Second, if you are worried about disengaging from someone, **you are making assumptions** about them. You are putting your thoughts into their heads. What you feel might be a crushing rejection for them, they might see as just part of the evening.

Third, if you have been following the Flirtology tenets, then **you haven't 'led them on'**. You have asked them a question, assessed, asked them a question, assessed. At some point, you have realized this is not working for you. You have not gone in all guns blazing, making outlandish promises and flinging yourself at them. You have had a conversation.

Fourth, **how 'kind' are you really being** by not bringing an end to the conversation when you have had enough? Think of the example above. My friend felt she was doing the right thing by spending time talking with Tim in the kitchen. But what in reality was she doing to him? She had realized her lack of romantic feelings early on. And half an hour later, she had lost all interest. From that point on, all she was doing was soaking up his time – time that he could have better spent trying to make a real connection with someone else. You aren't doing anyone a favour by prolonging an encounter that isn't working.

Finally, **be honest with yourself**. Too often we don't disentangle ourselves from others because we are using them as a safety raft, someone to cling on to so we won't be cast out there all alone until someone else comes along. That's not really about being kind, is it?

How to disengage

So, those are the theoretical reasons why you shouldn't have any difficulty in simply bringing to an end an encounter that has run its course. In practice, what should you actually say? Do you need to fake the sudden onset of a rare disease, catch a friend's eye, pretend your phone is ringing and make a swift exit stage-left?

No. An all-purpose 'It was nice to meet you, I hope you enjoy the rest of the evening' should suffice. It's clear and it's friendly. If they insist on continuing and show no signs of letting you go, then you might need to repeat it or vary it: 'I'm going to go and mingle for a bit – have a great evening.'

People seem to have this notion that if you make an exit, then you have to physically leave the event. Clients have told me that after disengaging with someone they then had to creep around the edges of the party pretending to be invisible or, even worse, actually leave an event for fear of encountering the person again. You are allowed to end a conversation. You don't have to pretend to disappear!

Accepting the signals

While most of the population is mortified at being seen as pushy or invading others' space, there is a smaller group of people who refuse to take a clear statement at face value. Don't be one of them. Not long ago, a friend and I were out at a wine bar. On a trip to refresh our drinks, a couple of guys came up to me: 'Can you tell me what the best wines are? We don't know much about them.' Good approach, I thought to myself. I wish more people would do this. We chatted for a few minutes about the advantages of the Godella grape. And then I signalled that the encounter was over: 'Well, I must leave now. My friend is waiting for her drink. I hope you enjoy my recommendation and have a nice evening.' Up to this point, everything was going according to the Flirtology philosophy: engaging in conversation, finding commonality and then saying that it's been nice, but it's now over.

And I returned to our table. Ten minutes later, my friend and I were heads together, intent on catching up and deep in the middle of a story. No signals of approachability here. So, when the guy and his friend were headed our way, I noticed out of the corner of my eye and deliberately didn't make eye contact, hoping he'd get the message. He didn't. This time when he approached, he was interrupting us. I told him in a friendly way that we were deep in the middle of something and that we were out together for a catch-up.

'So, you are telling us to get lost then?' he said.

'Well, I wouldn't have phrased it quite like that, but sure.'

Thirty minutes later, guess who showed up again? (His friend had enough sense not to join him.) And his gambit this time was enough to sink the heart of even the most cheerful flirter. 'I was taught that it's a man's job to hassle women.'

Now, I don't know who has been teaching him, but I wish they would stop. Because that is not how you flirt! (Funnily enough, his attitude would have been very familiar to anyone who has been out on the flirting scene in New York. This wasn't necessarily the situation in our case, but the attitude over there is that good-looking women will have a host of men after them, trying to get their attention, and that only the persistent will succeed. In my opinion, it's something that has the potential to ruin many a good night out.)

We have much to learn from this encounter. He started off with a good approach and, even though he was flirting up the wrong tree, the interaction had been positive, until he drove it into the ground.

So, let's re-cap on the Flirtology advice for these situations:

1. If someone has the courage to come up to you, treat him or her nicely. We want to encourage more people to interact with each other. It won't happen if we give them negative reactions.

2. If it's you who wants to approach someone, watch the body-language and eye-contact cues. Look for people who have open body language. They are more likely to be open to conversation. Closed body language and no looking around means that people are not open to conversation.

3. No means no. Always. And we should be attuned to receiving that signal not just through words but also by understanding others' signals of approachability.

4. Just because someone has come up to you doesn't mean that you have to spend time speaking with him or her. Except for common decency towards other humans, you don't 'owe' anyone anything. A graceful exit can be employed, and no one should ever feel trapped in a conversation. When you are done, you are done.

4. The green light

But enough of the negative vibes. Let's talk about success – most importantly, yours! You spot someone across the room. You both give a flicker of eye contact, enough that when the person comes to stand near you, you are filled with a little rush of excitement. They have now moved to the bar and are ordering a drink. You take your opportunity. You stand next to them and say, 'What's the drink of choice around here?' They smile and respond. From here, it just keeps getting better. You both love Spanish Rioja, have done half-marathons but also enjoy rainy days with a good book. You are surreptitiously edging closer as you speak. Lots of smiling and eye contact. There have definitely been some light taps on the arm. H.O.T. A.P.E. signals have all been ticked off. This is going well . . .

But suddenly it's going too well. Oh no. The nerves are starting to kick in. How do you move it on without blowing it?

First, be aware that you don't have to do anything *in that moment* except enjoy yourself. **Pay attention to the natural flow of the conversation** and the context in which you are having it. If you've fallen into conversation at the bar, for instance, your encounter is going to have a natural stopping point; you can't camp out at the bar with drinks spilling all over you and both sets of friends frantically signalling their thirst from the other side of the room. But you might not want to suddenly blurt out a demand for a phone number either. This is fine. You can move away from someone without ending the whole thing: just **signal your intent**. 'I've got to get these drinks back to my friends, but I really hope I see you later' or 'This has been great. Perhaps I'll see you at the interval?' The point is to leave this encounter on an open, positive note to set yourself up for the next encounter. You can pick it up again later.

Don't ruin your flow with a constant pressure on yourself: 'How can I turn this into a date?'; 'How can I make sure he's actually into me?'; 'How can I ensure that this person will become the mother of my future children?' If you are enjoying the encounter and they are too, then that is all we are looking for in that moment. Allow yourself to revel in it. Or as one of my NY interviewees put it: 'Sometimes the flirt is enough.'

And sometimes the flirt might be enough; you don't always have to be getting dates or digits. But if what you are looking for is something more – and that is what this book is all about – then you have to be bold. This is where you need to step up. You need to let the person know that you are interested.

Now, this is the point at which I find many people get nervous. So far, the Flirtology philosophy has been gentle, step by step, pressure-free. And now I'm telling you that you have to show your hand, to let them know that you are properly interested in them: you have romantic intentions. This can sound frightening, especially to people who would rather do almost anything than admit to someone they find them attractive. But there's a reason why I described this as 'being bold' rather than 'being brave'. Because actually, there's nothing to be brave about. *Why* does this feel frightening? What is there to be afraid of?

For a start, what you are offering them is a compliment: you like them, you want to get to know them better. Just as we have seen with offering people a smile, they can do as they want with it. What's the worst that could happen? An imbalance between how attractive you find them and how attractive they find you? Well, we know that rejection is not something to fear; it's a useful tool to filter out those who won't be a good match. If you make your interest in someone clear and they don't reciprocate, that is fine. This is about finding a good match, not trying to rack up a list of people who find you hot. The mental model here should be: *'I find this person attractive, and I am not afraid to let them know it.'*

So, how do you show your interest?

You shouldn't be thinking, 'How can I make this person think *I'm* attractive?' but rather, 'How can I make this person feel special?'

This is where H.O.T. A.P.E. is once again your friend. Previously, you have used it to try to establish whether someone is interested in you. Now, you use it to show that you are interested in them! Specifically, the two heavyweights here to convey undeniable interest are **touch** and **eye contact**. These are the best weapons in your flirting arsenal, but the full H.O.T. A.P.E. should come into play.

Humour lets you work out if the person is a good fit for you, and the very act of laughing releases endorphins in the brain, causing us – and them – to feel good. And the power of endorphins is nothing to laugh at. Anthropologist Robin Dunbar of the University of Oxford says, 'We think that it is the bonding effects of the endorphin rush that explain why laughter plays such an important role in our social lives.' If you want to attract them with humour, can I suggest making a joke about chickens crossing roads? There is nothing funnier. Trust me.

You should be making sure your body language is **open**. You might be feeling anxious and cross your arms across your chest as a subconscious gesture of self-comfort. But while you're reassuring yourself, the other person is interpreting it as 'go away'. Not the message that you wanted to send, right?

Touch is, as we have seen, a great signifier. It creates feelings in the other person even at a physiological level, and it demonstrates that you are, undeniably, interested. (A good thing, remember?) But you have to use touch wisely. This isn't an open invitation to start groping people. You need to be aware of which zones on the body are flirtatious fun and which are completely off limits. Broadly, the arms, the shoulders and back are all good. For the rest, wait for an invitation. As a general rule, a friendlier touch is on the shoulder or high up on the arm. The closer towards your hand, the flirtier the feeling. If you do want to show interest, lightly tap someone's hand as you give them a compliment. Or gently touch their lower back as you move past them; if you are walking behind them, you can gently touch their lower back to signify to them that you are right there with them. When you get up from the table, you could put a hand on their upper back as you lean down, look them in the eyes and tell them you'll return soon.

To be clear, I don't want to hear reports about you randomly touching people up. Touch is powerful when used correctly, but it can go very wrong when not. Which is why you need to be sensitive to the situation. If you are already in a bit of steamy banter, then, yes, touch their hand to make it flirtier. But if you haven't built up the rapport yet, desist. This is the line. Touch works best to escalate something that is already there. It's used to build upon the attraction but not as a starting point. As always: test, then assess. In that space of assessment, you can see if your touch is well received. Often, they will reciprocate if they liked it or smile at you.

Make sure you are giving the other person your full **attention**. Sometimes, when we get nervous, we are so intent on making ourselves feel more comfortable by doing things such as crossing our arms or giving the other person broken eye contact as we dart our eyes around the room, that it makes the other person feel that we are not really concentrating on them. Allow them to see that you want to hear what they say. Remember, you are trying to make them feel special.

Proximity is another powerful signal, as we know. If you want to indicate interest, make sure you're standing close enough for the possibility of whispering sweet nothings into their ear at some point. But it's another tricky one to get right because people can have different preferences around personal space depending on a number of variables: culture, gender, height, number of siblings, mood and attraction to you. Some people can be touchy about their personal space. As one female interviewee from New York said, 'They are in your personal space. You either mind or you don't.' This is why participant observation is a useful tool. By all means lean in, but keep an eye out for their reaction and adjust accordingly.

As for **eye contact**, we don't want you suddenly to start trying to hypnotize the other person. Like touch, eye contact is part of a continuum – the glance across the room, the mingling of gazes as you fall into conversation. By this point, you should be looking directly at the other person. Usually, the listener will make eye contact with the speaker 100 per cent of the time, and the speaker will make eye contact around 80 per cent, throwing in an occasional look to the side now and again but then quickly returning the gaze. You probably do this naturally anyway. The steamier the encounter gets, the more the eye contact becomes 100 per cent focused on each other.

H.O.T. A.P.E. in action

H.O.T. A.P.E. has an extra benefit. It helps turn flirting into a benign game, something fun. This can take the pressure off. One of my clients told me that she and her friends had been out the previous night. One of the friends gathered her courage and said, 'I'm going to go H.O.T. A.P.E. that guy.' (See, it's even a verb.) She returned a few moments later slightly despondent – 'He wasn't interested.'

'Well,' my client asked, 'did you H.O.T. A.P.E. him?'

'I think so . . .'

'Did you say anything funny to break the ice?'

'Yes, I think so.'

'You didn't do your arm-cross thing, did you?'

'No, I made sure my arms were open.'

'What about touch? Did you touch his arm?'

She thinks for a moment and then smiled, 'No, I didn't do the arm touch. No wonder!'

And then they both started laughing. Suddenly, what might have felt like soul-destroying rejection was now just a fun game, where you forgot to make a move and so you didn't 'win'.

The magic words

H.O.T. A.P.E. covers the unspoken gestures that signal your interest. But of course what you talk about comes into play here too. It might sound obvious, but when flirting consider the subject of your conversation as well as the physical cues. As one of my research interviewees put it, 'If they're flirting with you, they're not going to be talking about the weather.' Remember, you are not aiming for a conversation that makes them think *you* are more attractive but one that makes *them* feel attractive.

There are two ways of making the other person feel attractive. The most obvious is **compliments**. And because you're a smart person, I am sure you will pick it up quickly. (Yes, that was a compliment.)

The point of compliments is that they should arise out of the specific moment and feel both genuine and spontaneous. Therefore, the compliments that I have given you below will sound cheesy in this context – you have been warned. I just wanted to give you some examples of what I mean. You can adapt them to fit your situation. These are the key principles for giving a good compliment:

1. If you find someone attractive, you are going to be thinking nice things about them – about their smile, their eyes, their sharp sense of humour. Why not tell them? The tendency is to stop ourselves. Don't. Just say it out loud. 'You have such a wonderful smile. It makes me think you are up to something mischievous.'

2. Compliments only work if they are genuine. Say what you mean. 'I love your take on things. It's really refreshing.'

3. Part of appearing genuine is giving a compliment that is specific to the person. 'You have nice eyes' could equally be said to your pet parrot. Therefore, it doesn't serve the job of making someone feel special. Instead try, 'I am sorry, can you repeat that? I was so busy looking at your eyes that I momentarily lost track of the conversation.'

4. The point of a compliment is to make someone feel good, not embarrassed. If you are complimenting someone's body, stick to non-specific body parts, like, 'That dress shows off your amazing figure' or 'You look very handsome tonight.'

Some people say that they feel uncomfortable being on the receiving end of compliments. If this sounds like you, think about why you feel that way. Why does someone saying something nice about you make you feel uncomfortable? What about looking at it from another perspective? Receiving a compliment is like receiving a gift; if someone tried to give you a gift, would you reject it? So, why would you do the same with a compliment? And as for *how* you receive a compliment? All you have to do is smile and say, 'Thank you.'

Besides compliments, the other thing you are trying to do in order to make the other person feel special is to **create a shared space**. The way to do this is to use inclusive language: 'we' and 'us'. For example, 'We should go get another drink' or 'We have the same sense of humour.' 'People like us will always . . .' You will already have been trying to find areas of common interest with the other person, so what you are now looking to do is to take those shared areas and build on them so that they become something you share *together*. Using inclusive language, with the addition of genuine compliments, is how you get to know someone as a potential partner and not just a friend.

Showing your hand

At some point, any encounter will have to wind down. And if you want to see them again, you will have to put yourself on the line and **ask them**. For some people, this feels scary no matter how well the conversation has been going.

Showing your hand can be done in two ways:

First, remember the social contagion effect? People are most open and positive when they are talking about something they love. I hope you've been working that principle into your conversation and discussing your shared enthusiasms. If so, just **link your next encounter to something that they feel passionate about**. 'I rarely meet anyone who shares my love of Nouvelle Vague cinema. There's a great film showing at the Rialto theatre. Do you want to go next week?' Or 'I loved hearing about your capoeira classes. Do they accept beginners? Maybe I could join you sometime.' I found this a common theme among the people I spoke to who knew how to move things on successfully: 'Concentrate on the things you are both interested in and build on that,' as one flirter in Stockholm put it.

My favourite example of this came from one of my flirting tours. As usual, I'd taken a group to a supermarket and asked them to use the food items as props to start a conversation with a stranger. One woman found herself in the rice aisle with a cute guy, asking advice about the best rice to use for making a curry. It turned out he was a curry aficionado. And after an enthusiastic conversation about the merits of basmati, he'd suggested they move the conversation on from the supermarket to somewhere a bit spicier, his favourite Indian restaurant. The last I heard they were dallying over dahl.

The other way to show your interest is to be **direct**. It doesn't need to be convoluted or fancy. No flash mob required. Just say what you feel: 'This is the best conversation I've had in so long. Would you like to do it again sometime?'

 How to extend an invitation

A good flirtatious encounter involves an air of the unknown. At this moment in time, neither of you know what will happen yet or what you will be to each other: a new friend, great sex, life partners or just the fun of the flirt. But, if you are interested in seeing them again, the way you extend an invitation can tell the other person a lot. A friendly invite would be to invite them to join your tennis group. A flirty invite would be to invite them to play one-on-one. Any time you bring in other people to the invite, it makes it look like your intentions are just friendly. One of my male clients showed me a text he wrote to a woman. He started out great. He asked her if she would like to join him for a drink at the weekend. But, at the very end, he chickened out. His last line was, 'I will see if some of the others want to join as well.' In one fell swoop, and as a perceived measure of safety, he went from making his intentions clear, to making everything very confusing. On another note, if you were interested in getting to know someone

167

better, you could specifically organize a group event and then contact them to ask if they were going to be there. Do you see the difference?

So, now you know what to do in each of the following scenarios: determining friendly or flirting interest, the knock-back, making a graceful exit or the green light. So, grab your shoes. It's time to get out there, because your next move is to get yourself into one of these situations. From there, you can practise identifying which category your encounters fit into and then trying each of them out. Now, all we need to do is find the people to practise on.

6

Where Do I Find Them?

I RECENTLY GAVE a flirting masterclass to an audience of over a hundred people. Afterwards, most of us went downstairs to the bar for more practice. A man came up to me at the bar with a huge smile on his face. 'This class was a life-changer for me. I loved it.' I always try to meet as many people as I can before the talk starts, and I remembered him from the pre-class meet-up. He had spent most of the time standing alone in the corner interacting with only his phone. So, the possibility that the next time he was surrounded by a hundred other single people he might not dive straight into his screen was pleasing to hear.

He continued, 'There's just one thing, though. It strikes me that you don't like the online world very much. But I think you're wrong. I live my life online: I shop there, I work there, I socialize there, I network there. I don't see why all your principles of Flirtology can't apply there as well. I can flirt with people and put at least five of the six H.O.T. A.P.E. principles into practice there just as well as in the offline world. So, why can't a digitally oriented person like me just do all my Flirtology stuff online?'

My immediate reaction was that a wink emoji is just not the same as two people eyeing each other up across a crowded room, and never will be. But he had caught my attention. I like to think I have an open mind, and the possibility that I could be completely missing something intrigued me. The situation also reminded me of something that had happened when I was researching flirting in Stockholm. I had been interviewing Swedish people about how they used eye contact – in what situations, how well it worked; they all said that eye contact was a huge part of the flirting experience. But I had been in Sweden for a few weeks, and I had never observed anybody making flirtatious eye contact with anyone. Not on public transport, or in the shops, or anywhere else that this flirting eye contact was purported to be happening. I knew there was only one thing to be done. I had to call on an anthropologist's favourite tool when she is in the field and things don't seem to be adding up: local knowledge. In this case, it came in the form of my two Swedish key informants – Christofer and Mattias. They did a role play with me and demonstrated what Swedish eye contact looked like. It was so slight that we had to do it twice. What I thought was someone blinking in my vicinity was actually a Swede making eye contact with me. The point is that it wasn't registering as eye contact because it didn't look like it to me. I had to tune in to what *they* meant by eye contact in order to see it. Was the world of digital flirting just like Stockholm all over again? Was there something here that I simply wasn't seeing?

In fact, I was so intrigued that I decided to meet the guy again to investigate further. We sat down the following week to thrash out what he thought digital-world flirting brought to the Flirtology party. He raised some interesting points. For example, he didn't see any particular division between the online world and the offline. For him, the two melded together. For me, the two are distinct, and I use the online world to aid my real-world experiences. Our varying viewpoints about how we each inhabit these worlds was present even in the language we both chose to describe things. He didn't like my use of the phrase 'real world' because it implied that he wasn't in the real world when he was online. I objected to using the phrase 'offline', because it implies that online is the default mode and everything else is compared to that. Regardless, he reasoned that it makes sense for him to practise Flirtology principles in both. And with this I agree to an extent. The online world is part of our lives now, and I am not here to change your mind about it. I'd be a hypocrite; I haven't actually done a weekly shop in a supermarket in over five years. Thank you, supermarket app!

I am also completely on board with the idea that the digital world is filled with a myriad of useful tools for communication. Why wouldn't you make the most of them? Met someone at a works drinks whose email address you never got? Of course use LinkedIn to try to re-open the connection. Talked to a really intriguing artist at a gallery opening? Then by all means follow them on Instagram. Swapped numbers with a cute girl at a party?

Then, yes, choose your medium: Facebook, Twitter, Snapchat, WhatsApp, WeChat. There are a million ways for the internet to help you reconnect with people and even prolong the frisson that comes with an excellent flirtatious interaction.

It's even possible to go a little further: Flirtology is about **maximizing flirting opportunities**. If those opportunities happen to arise online because you naturally spend a lot of your time there, there's no reason to ignore them. Obviously, one must use some sense when dealing with the digital world. In what other forum in our lives do people have the option of ranting, raving, inciting and, much rarer, complimenting, all under the protective guise of 'anonymous'? (I can't believe this is still even an option!) However, if you're on a trusted and safe internet forum that you habitually frequent, and you find yourself agreeing with every word someone types, and you have even exchanged some invaluable words of wisdom via Instant Messenger, well, it is possible to suggest meeting up in person to discuss more. (Preferably not in a dark alley or someone's home. We are looking to meet potential love interests, not axe-murderers.) One of the sweetest news stories that caught my eye in recent years was a love story about a circus performer who married her dream man: a bookseller whose humorous book-lover's Twitter feed she had been following for ages. It sounds like a rom-com come true, the ultimate meet-cute moment.

But this is not really an internet love story at all. It was only when she stepped out of his virtual world and into the real one that anything sparked up. She kept trying to cast out lures on Twitter to no avail; it was only when she turned up at his workplace with a bag of doughnuts that things actually took off. In a *Guardian* interview about their romance, she described Twitter as: 'It's how we started, but it's not integral to anything.'

And this exemplifies where I found myself diverging from my new friend, the digital ambassador. Because where he believed that the best kind of internet encounter could encapsulate all the thrills of flirting, I don't think it comes anywhere close. All the online forums and WhatsApp messages don't have a hope of matching the real thing. As we learned earlier, studies have shown that online social contacts are 'not an effective alternative for offline social interactions'. The internet, with all its means of communication, is a tool, nothing more; it's not a substitute for real-world experience.

It is also a tool which shouldn't be used mindlessly. It's too easy to fall down the rabbit hole of online communication without stopping to get our bearings. We are presented with an alluring cocktail of constant stimulation and mindlessness. The psychologist Adam Alter points out that our interaction with screens now lacks 'stopping cues'. Until recently, we have used media such as books, films, newspapers or TV programmes, which all come with natural stopping points: the programme ends, the chapter finishes, the credits come up. But the digital world is bottomless: you can keep scrolling and clicking forever. The scattergun nature of our concentration online can mean that our flirtatious energies get dissipated and wasted. Conversations can ping back and forth without any particular resolution. Fun for a while and great if it gives you a kick – in fact, internet traffic is designed that way, using something called 'captology'. Apps generate small habitual behaviours, such as swiping right or counting 'likes', that are designed to produce ephemeral dopamine bursts. The combination of physiological and behavioural effects is mighty powerful stuff – guaranteed to keep bringing you back for more – but not necessarily a great way to find love.

If you are in the throes of virtual flirtation, it's worth stopping for a moment to consider what you are doing. You could ask yourself the following questions:

- How much time am I spending here?
- Is this bringing me closer to what I want?
- Am I doing this for the right reason?
- Is this making me feel good?
- If it used to feel good, is it still feeling good?

Check in with yourself frequently. Ask yourself these questions regularly. Interactions online can change with a ping.

Digital apes

My digital ambassador friend was firmly of the opinion that all the signifiers of flirting that H.O.T. A.P.E. encapsulates (barring touch) were just as relevant online. He felt you could get just as good a sense of a successful flirtatious encounter in the virtual world. But I don't agree. For example, the 'H' in H.O.T. A.P.E. stands for humour. You may laugh uproariously at someone's text witticisms or admire their perfectly timed, perfectly elegant tweet. But this isn't the same as sharing their sense of humour. How much of this will translate into real life? If you met this person in the real world, would the sharp wit turn into a red flag for a pessimistic, negative grouch? And how long does it take that person to come up with each brilliant aperçu? When you read that wry voice online, how much of the humour are you actually supplying yourself? And what of the opposite? The person whose charm and wit might be readily obvious when you meet them but whose skills don't extend to expressing their personality in a limited number of characters? Does this person not even feature, then?

The 'A' in H.O.T. A.P.E. stands for attention, and this is another thing you can't get an accurate reading of online. You simply can't gauge how much attention is being focused on you from a virtual interaction. It may feel special, and your phone may be buzzing in your pocket from the number of incoming messages, but, for all you know, that person who is so avidly DMing you is simultaneously doing the same to three other people or is just bored, idling away some time on a commute. In a face-to-face encounter, being the recipient of someone's attention *is* special. It's a gift. You know that it's all for you. You don't have to compete with a dancing Jimmy Fallon gif while someone orders new shoes.

My digital ambassador made the case that the virtual world is visually led. In his view, eye contact could be simulated on the internet by the fact that people bring themselves into your vision by engaging with you. For example, liking something that someone posted would bring you to their attention. You would visually be on their radar. To me, this is no substitute for the electricity that comes when you and the attractive stranger across the room lock eyes. No developer could ever create anything that stimulates a dopamine burst like this. Or what about the dilation of the pupils as your attraction builds when you are in a face-to face-encounter, all systems alight, from the body to the brain?

It's impossible to accurately judge the *quality* of an interaction online. What the internet does offer us is *quantity*: as my new friend put it, 'You can meet fifty women online in five minutes. Timewise, it's a better return on investment.' But is it? When you start with such a large funnel, it takes a lot of time to whittle things down. Not to mention, quantity of encounters is not the same as quality interactions. Is this really a good use of time?

The only view you can get of anyone online is a narrow one: usually a carefully presented facade that highlights only certain characteristics. Likewise, communication online is more one-dimensional as well. Let's say that you are engaging in a witty tête-à-tête with someone online. Great, how fun! Keep those keys a whizzing. Now, let's say you are engaging in a witty tête-à-tête with someone at your local coffee shop. Soon, that mutual laughter might add to prolonged eye contact. This might lead to a playful touch on the arm. This might lead to two bodies moving closer together. From here, anything could happen. At least, much more than it could between you and your keyboard. Because communication online is linear. Digital flirting is not about two people creating something together but, rather, each person taking a turn and then the other responding. It's almost impossible to build layers, and it is the building up of these layers that makes for a genuine connection.

The only way you can find out all the layers and nuances of a person is by seeing them face to face. By all means use virtual tools to keep the fizz of an initial flirtation going, but if you are looking for more than a video-game girlfriend, you must both step out from behind your screens and see what spark you have in the real world.

How to step out from the screen

It is all too easy to find that what looked like a promising start tails off into a string of messages, texts and online interaction that feels thrilling at first but never really leads anywhere. The back-and-forth of virtual conversation can be fun, but if it's ever going to lead to something solid, you need to make sure you take that thrill into the real world, pronto.

To avoid being caught in this limbo, be firm and proactive.

- Be aware of how much time and emotional energy you are pouring into this online conversation. Is it getting in the way of your real socializing and flirting opportunities?
- Give yourself a deadline that fits well with your life. For instance, if your avid mutual messaging hasn't solidified into plans to meet by the second week, do something about it.
- As in the offline world, either party can and should take the initiative.
- The same rules apply online as offline. Remember your deal-breakers. Do they fulfil them? In

particular, can you actually meet them in person? There's no point having a great conversation, with the hope of more, with someone halfway around the world.

- Don't get sucked into thinking you know this person better than you do just because you've been texting madly for two weeks.

My second concern about dating websites and apps stems from people's behaviour on them. More often I am hearing clients' stories of how somebody ghosted them or said they would call and never did. It's something people repeatedly ask me: why does there seem to be an epidemic of people saying they will do something and not doing it? If I ask them where they met this person, I am never surprised to find out it was online. There is no denying that when people are interacting in a space where there are no set codes of behaviour and almost no repercussions for one's actions, they *will* behave differently. Call it human nature.

If I introduce two friends in real life and one ghosts the other, I can assure you that they will have me to answer to for their behaviour. Not pretty. Or if you are set up on a date with your mother's friend's son or daughter, you had better believe that socially acceptable behaviour – heightened by the telling-off from one's mother – will affect the behaviour of both parties. But what if it's some person named John or Jane whom you met on an app? To them, your face is just one of hundreds that they have looked at in the last week. You have no friends in common and if either of you behaves badly there are practically zero repercussions. Is it surprising that sometimes manners and empathy fly out the window?

Think about it. In the real world, can people walk around anonymously? Hardly. It feels like quite the opposite. I need ID to buy sparklers. In the real world, can people assume a fake identity or just create one to suit their liking, with little hassle and no questioning? No, so why are we trying to find real love and make real connections in an environment where we are not required to be real at all? When we speak about 'people's behaviour' in the dating world, let's be clear that there is a distinction between how people act in the digital world – a place where being your true self is optional – and the real world.

I know that critical mass has been reached and there are more people using online dating and apps than ever before. And I can certainly see the seduction: it makes us feel like we are being proactive, it's convenient, it's easy, we can think of a clever retort without pressure from the comfort of our sofa, and our silver screens can, we think, protect us from rejection. But let me ask you one question: **is this giving you what you want?** If the answer is 'yes', wonderful. You can probably stop reading here. But if not, then read on.

The evolution of digital dating

Where were you when you used a computer for the first time? I was 11 years old. I used to play the game Oregon Trail in the library of my primary school. The computer was big, old, slow and clunky, and perfectly summed up our relationship with digital technology at that time. I refer to this as the *Pre-digital era* and if, like me, you were born in the seventies, you might have had similar experiences.

How old were you when you had your first email account? I was a freshman in college, 1992. I consider this the first phase of the *Desktop era*. Whilst I was delighted to not have to consult out-of-date encyclopedias as my main source of reference, my engagement with the digital world was still limited. My email address consisted of my university-provided email account, and I still had to go to the computer lab to access it. There wasn't much point in checking emails anyway, as no one ever used them. People still met in real life: at parties, bars, sporting events, etc.

Things started to change after my university graduation, which coincided with the emergence of the World Wide Web into the broader public domain. It was the beginning of chatrooms, MySpace and the first internet dating sites. It was the start of a huge shift which began bringing our real-world communities online. It also began to alter how we meet. This is the era when online flirting first started to become a thing. I consider this phase the *Desktop 2.0 era.*

However, the era which arguably caused the biggest change in behaviour and brought us where we are today is the *Mobile era*. Apple brought out its iPhone in 2007, which was followed by the first Android-powered phones the following year. Smartphones went from 10 per cent to 40 per cent market penetration faster than any other consumer technology in history. In the United States, adoption hit 50 per cent only three years ago; imagine, a decade ago almost no one had a smartphone.

How has this affected the dating scene?

Pre-digital era: we went out to parties, talked to people.

Desktop 2.0 era: we met people in internet chatrooms. There were no real criteria for matching with people, beyond having common interests and liking the way they expressed themselves. You might have started an email relationship. It might have been weeks before you knew what the other person looked like, if they even agreed to send you a photo. The attitude of this era was: 'I am talking to a guy. I hope he is cute!'

Then came online dating. Now there were lots of criteria – tick boxes to check off and photos to choose from. In this era, the attitude was: 'I like his profile. Should I speak with him?' There were also lots of barriers to communication: possibly paying for membership, sorting through profiles, reading and constructing messages.

Mobile era (present day): only three criteria points are needed: picture, height and weight. No need to use critical thinking or any filtering mechanisms. People are presented solely in a physical way. Therefore, the question becomes different. It's now: 'He's hot. Should I sleep with him?' People can be accessed immediately. No waiting around required. And this immediate access brings with it less patience and more expectation.

Is this all progress? You decide.

So, where to find them?

If I'm banning you from using dating apps and urging caution about meeting people online, then it's pretty reasonable for you to ask me where you're supposed to find people to flirt with.

The short answer to this is – everywhere. I can hear your groan from here. I knew you were waiting for the secret address, the one where you open the door and all of your Mr and Ms Rights are waiting there for you with open arms. Sorry, there is no such place. (But there *is* a Santa Claus, so it all evens out.) However, once you have brought the Flirtology principles into your life, then you should be seeing opportunities every day: from the grocery store to your workplace.

But I can also see that this feels a little simplistic: not everybody lives in a neighbourhood where the local coffee-shop guy is perfect for them or where their ideal woman is sitting on the 8.45 train every morning. You may feel you want more practical tips. So, here are your two best friends: the principles of **commonality** and **proximity**.

Commonality

Commonality is a simple tool but an effective one. And it's probably something you are using already (though you may not have thought about it in this way). One of the first things we tend to do when meeting someone new is to start finding commonality with them – what sports teams do they support, where did they grow up, do you have any mutual friends?

It's not a radical idea to believe that a key component in our partner search is finding people with whom we share things in common. But to make the most out of this principle, I want to make sure you are doing this proactively and systematically.

First, **make sure that you are doing the things that make you happy,** that fulfil you and your needs in life. You look for places and activities not because you think they are going to be fertile hunting grounds for singletons but because they reflect who you are and what you like to do. This means that your life is not some big quest to find a partner, which often gives off vibes of desperation and neediness. But, rather, you are out living an interesting, well-rounded life. You are taking the responsibility for making your life good, not looking for someone to fill in the gaps for you.

Next, **think about the points in your life that bring you into contact with others**: your work, your social life, your hobbies, your passions. Are you making the most of these? Are you missing opportunities for flirtation? For example, are there people in your work environment – the office canteen, the next floor up, networking events – whom you have vaguely noticed but allowed to fade into the background?

Use your interests to the full: think about what you like to do in your free time. If the answer is lying on the sofa watching Netflix, you might want to reassess. You could join a film club instead – the same entertainment, same access to comfy seats, with the possibility of meeting fellow fans. If your hobbies feel as if they are solitary, look at whether they can be more social: join book clubs, running clubs, evening classes. Look at local teams. I play on a softball team in the park, and I am always one of the few females.

So far, so easy. But we all probably have had the experience of joining a class or a group and not really meeting anyone there. That is because finding the group is just the first, obvious step.

The most important shift is in your own attitude and behaviour. I once joined a tennis weekend with two of my female clients who were looking for romantic partners. I thought a weekend in the park playing tennis would be fun. As we were having coffee at the end of the weekend, I asked them if they had met anyone nice. They said it had been great, but they hadn't met anyone single. 'You mean you didn't meet Alex?' I asked. They shook their heads, 'Who's Alex?' Not only had I met the lovely, single Alex, but I also had his number and had arranged for us all to play doubles together the next weekend. Why hadn't *they* met Alex?

This is the most important point: **commonality will not work unless you make it work for you**. And this means a change in your own behaviour. It's no good just being in a place with other people who share your interests. You need to also be open – open-minded, open in your body language, open to engaging with others. And this has to be a conscious, active state.

You cannot go into environments hoping, in a passive way, that everyone will just come running over to you with big smiles and arms wide open. Because this means you will always be left standing in the corner, fervently wishing that someone might come and speak to you. If you don't take the initiative, you run the risk of everyone else doing the same thing: waiting in their corners hoping for you to make the move. Result: stasis. It's a lot more fun – and more effective – to be proactive and make the approaches. You might not know where it will lead, but it's you who is making things happen.

One of my male clients used to go on solo runs. Wanting to meet more people, he joined a running club. But he didn't just join it. He followed all the Flirtology principles: showed up early, talked to lots of people before the runs started, showed his face enough to become familiar, and moved into the proximity of people whom he found attractive. He now has a regular run with one of the women, à deux.

The beauty of using commonality in your partner search is that it becomes a part of your daily life. You don't have to visit special places, wear special clothes or behave in a certain way. You just do what you are already doing but in a smarter way. You live your life but with your eyes open to the opportunities around you.

Not long ago, I went to a lecture with a friend. Before we took a seat, I looked around to see if there were any cute guys sitting alone. I corralled her near an interesting-looking guy, and we sat down. I realized it was likely that the speaker would ask us to introduce ourselves to our neighbours at some point in the pro-ceedings, so since I happened to be sitting next to the man, I suggested to her that we swap seats 'so she could see better'. And, sure enough, at the beginning of the talk we all had to turn to our neighbour and say hello. This established a connection between my friend and the guy that made it easy for them to pick up a con-versation during the interval while I went off to get the drinks. As soon as the lecture was over, I made an excuse to go to the loo, returning to join my friend once I knew they would have had enough time to swap numbers. As I joined them again, I heard her say, 'Well, if you give me your email, I can send you more information about that author we were discussing.' This must be what proud parents feel like. 'Isn't it amazing?' she said as we left. 'So lucky I happened to sit next to such a great guy . . .'

What have we learned from this story other than the fact that I am the world's best wing-woman? With a few simple steps, you too can create such 'miraculous' results. But it is up to you to create the situation: sitting next to the person who has caught your eye, detaching yourself from a larger group to talk to one person alone, asking questions, exchanging contact details, seizing opportunities. My friend conveyed to me that the guy replied to her email asking her out and remarking that he 'must find out more about why the two of them, out of everyone there, had been seated next to each other'. Oh, brother, not him too.

Proximity

Proximity is another obvious but underused tool. It's the reason why you probably have a better relationship with the person who sits next to you at work than you do with the people on the third floor. It won't surprise you to learn that physical closeness leads to psychological closeness and that proximity has been proven to be important when looking for potential partners. You have to interact with a person to figure out if you want to have a closer relationship with them, and proximity enables this.

The mere exposure effect

You see the same faces every day on your commute to work. You catch glimpses of people who look familiar as you do your weekly shopping at your neighbourhood grocery store. If asked, would you say that you like these faces? Or even prefer them to faces that you see for the first time? Psychologists say that you would.

Research by Bob Zajonc demonstrates that this is all due to our cognitive system, which uses familiarity as a way to judge that something is safe.

If you are exposed to something unpleasant, then you have a negative reaction to it. The cognitive system stores information about these unpleasant experiences, so the next time you encounter that thing again, you immediately get a signal to avoid it. For example, let's say you meet an arrogant loudmouth at a party. If you see said loudmouth again, you will avoid them at all costs. Why? Because you will experience an unpleasant feeling upon seeing them. Conversely, if you are exposed to something that is not unpleasant, like the nice-looking suit on your morning commute, then the cognitive system assumes that it is safe. The next time you encounter said suit, you will like him better than you did the first time. That is the cognitive system's way of telling you that it thinks that the item is safe. And makes your 8 a.m. haze a tiny bit more tolerable.

Sounds plausible. But how can psychologists examine this? One set of researchers arranged for four different women (of similar appearance) to attend a college class a certain number of times throughout the semester. One of these women didn't actually attend at all, one attended five times, one attended ten times, and the last woman attended fifteen times. These women didn't interact with the students at all; they just sat in on the lecture.

At the end of the semester, the students in the class saw pictures of each of the women and rated them on several scales such as physical attractiveness. Despite never having interacted with these women, the students showed a clear mere exposure effect. That is, they evaluated the woman whom they had seen 15 times much more positively than the woman they hadn't seen at all.

It is amazing what the brain does without us knowing. But what does this mean for you and your flirting life? It means that simply being seen by others can be a powerful tool. The more times you can make yourself known to another (without being too pushy, obviously), the more you can increase favourable feelings towards you. For example, if you make a point of making eye contact and smiling at someone when they enter a room, by the time you go up and ask them a question, they will already feel like they slightly know you, giving you the advantage over everyone else. Or you can say hi and smile at people on your weekly shop or at your local cafe. The next time you see them you will already have started the rapport-building process simply because they have already been exposed to that gorgeous mug of yours.

As we have seen from the mere exposure effect, just seeing a person a lot can lead you to like them more. It is those people whom we have seen before, who feel most familiar to us, that we warm to. In fact, most college friendships develop between people who live near to each other; those living close to stairwells and mailboxes (i.e. gathering places) became the most popular residents. So, what does this mean for you and utilizing proximity?

The trick is to build up a relationship with the world directly around you. One of my favourite places, which encapsulates both commonality and proximity, is one's very own neighbourhood. Get into the mindset of 'local' – your favourite coffee shop, your favourite local bar, the nearby park, that bookshop down the road. Find places you genuinely like and would frequent anyway. This gives you the opportunity to become a known face. If you really like your area, join neighbourhood associations, get involved in the local community. Volunteer to help run street parties. All these things can potentially embed you in a new social circle and bring you together with people with whom you probably share things in common.

Often when I give this advice to people they counter it by saying that they don't really like the area they live in. They live there for convenience, or they are about to move on. This is fine. Look at a nearby area that encapsulates the qualities you want: go to that bookshop in the next town, drive to the park that you really like to walk in, not just the one that happens to be on your doorstep. It's what you do whilst in these places that matters the most.

You are never going to meet that cute person in the local coffee shop if every time you go in there you dash to the counter, mumble your order, retreat to a corner seat and bury your head in a news-paper. The same rules of engagement apply at every flirting opportunity: look around, make sure your body language is open, keep your head up, smile and engage with people. If you see an interesting person in there, sit close to them, so that it feels natural when you lean over to ask them with a smile what the coffee is like.

Familiarity

Finally, look carefully at all the relationships you already have – with friends, with longstanding contacts and people you come into contact with in your day-to-day life. Are you missing any opportunities there? Without trying to turn you into a character in a rom-com, sometimes the people we are trying to attract in our lives are already there; it's just that we are not ready for them so we don't see them. I have lost count of the number of clients who come to me saying there is 'no one out there', but then re-examine their lives according to Flirtology principles and realize that actually they just haven't noticed some excellent opportunities. One of my clients was convinced that nobody found her attractive, and it wasn't until we looked into her life together that she suddenly realized that the man who ran the local bike shop, who kept asking her out for coffee, wasn't doing so because he had a caffeine addiction. He had been in her life all along, but a mixture of lack of confidence and habit had stopped her seeing him. They are now happily dating.

It can be hard to shift our vision, to think about people who have always been in the background of our lives and then suddenly move them into the spotlight. So, how do you go about viewing your familiar landscape through new lenses? The best thing to do is to return to your deal-breakers. You already have a list of the qualities you need in a partner. Do you know anyone who could possibly fulfil them? If so, is there anything in particular that is stopping you from finding out whether there might be more to your relationship than you had thought? This can feel alarming: you don't suddenly want to come on strong to someone whom you have known for a while. The stakes feel higher, the potential for embarrassment stronger. But remember: take a small step, assess. Take another one, assess.

The first step is to move to slightly different territory. If you only ever see each other for coffee at the gym, suggest meeting at the new cafe on the corner next time. If you only ever see someone in a large group, ask them if they'd like to do something with just the two of you. We're not talking about taking a big leap into a full-blown relationship. Just change your perspective and see where that leads you.

And that's what I did. I was my husband's Pilates teacher for a year. Every Thursday night, there he was, back left-hand corner. He seemed like a nice guy and would always say something witty as he put his mat away at the end of the class. But, for me, that was the extent of it. Until we started constantly bumping into each other. As the gym where I was teaching was local to both of us, we would also run into each other at the swimming pool at weekends and the supermarket and even on the street, until finally we said, almost in unison, 'We should meet up for a coffee sometime.' Did the mere exposure effect play Cupid for us? Was he only coming for the Pilates? I asked him once; he just gave me a wink and said how good Pilates had been for him.

Examine your opportunities

Think about your social life. Clients always tell me how busy their life is due to their constant socializing. But still, somehow, they never seem to meet anyone. It is only when we dig deeper that it becomes clear that this is part of the problem. Socializing is all very well, but if it's always with one tight group of friends or a dinner out with the same person from work, then the chances of meeting someone new or of giving yourself flirting opportunities can get very limited. As more than one previous client has realized, you can't continue doing what you have always done, going to the same places, hanging out with the same people, and expect the results to be different. It's time to shake things up!

It's also worth **enlisting your friends' help**. Let it be known you are looking to meet someone. Too many people assume that their friends know this. Don't assume anything. Your network is a great place to start. Roughly half of all relationships begin when individuals are introduced to each other by a mutual acquaintance, and two out of three people know members of their partner's social networks prior to meeting.

My other advice to people who feel that their social life has gotten into a rut is to **throw a party**. It's a wonderful opportunity to refresh connections and get to know people better who have been out on the periphery. If you feel you don't have the money or the space to be a gracious host, get creative: host picnics, gatherings in a bar, a BYOB event. Before you roll your eyes and think I am naive, just try it. Organizing an event gives you the opportunity to extend an invite to people whom you'd like to get to know better, and it's like giving someone a gift. They will feel special by being invited. Also, you have a built-in excuse at the party to speak with whomever you want. Tell me, what's not to like here?

Change your behaviour

In the end, the question isn't so much 'Where are all these people?' as 'Why aren't I finding them, and why aren't they finding me?' This was illustrated on a recent flirting tour. As the tour reached its conclusion, one of the women mentioned how lucky it was that there had been an equal number of men along and they all seemed 'so nice and normal'. 'Where are you guys usually hiding?' she joked. And so I asked each of the guys what they had been doing the previous weekend. The overriding answer was 'bars and pubs'. In other words, the same places that the women were hanging out. And I doubt that they were the only 'nice and normal' guys there. So, why weren't the women finding them? Because their own behaviour was getting in the way: going out in tight-knit groups, not looking around for people to meet and certainly not approaching them. No wonder they weren't meeting the nice guys. Remember what we said earlier. Just because you are in the vicinity of people with whom you might get on doesn't mean they will just fall into your lap. You need to be proactive here.

Make the most of your opportunities

One of the reasons that this whole dating thing might feel like a part-time job is because you are sectioning flirting off into a particular area of your life, done at particular times and places. One client told me about how she and her friend had decided to go to a singles' evening, hoping to possibly meet some nice guys. They met in the bar next door, where they happened to get talking to two nice guys, getting on well and laughing with them about what they were about to do. The guys suggested they skip the speed dating and just come out with them instead. But the girls felt committed: they had gotten themselves all ready for the event, paid for the tickets and didn't want to feel they were backing out of the 'dating' they had promised themselves they would do. So, they left *these* nice guys behind and went to their scheduled event to meet the 'nice guys' there. One guess if there was anyone there that they liked. They made a dash back to the bar, but the guys were gone . . .

Making a success of Flirtology means opening yourself up to all potential encounters and adjusting your behaviour so that opportunities don't pass you by. What does this look like when it works? A woman who came on my Fearless Flirting tour took this on board. Wanting to get out of her rut, she gave herself the challenge of making small changes to her social life to see what would happen. She mentioned that she and a friend liked to meet at a certain bar in their neighbourhood. I suggested turning up ten minutes early. She told me that her friend was always twenty minutes late, so that gave her plenty of time to case the place and look for opportunities. On her first attempt at trying things differently, she arrived early, chose a well-positioned table and then had a look around. When she spotted a good-looking guy standing at the bar, she went up to get herself a drink and placed herself next to him when ordering. And she used a classically Flirtology-esque line: 'You look like you're good in a dilemma. What should I have to drink?' She now informs me that they are going to be married this summer. All because she made a few small adjustments to her normal routine. The people you want to meet are all out there. What is getting in the way of you meeting them?

And when it comes to the digital world, just remember: it's a tool, not your answer to everything. In the end, I think even my digital ambassador friend would agree that there's nothing like the real world for making real connections. When I looked around that crowded bar for the last time before leaving my event, there he was, lips locked in an encounter with a fellow classmate. He might have been able to relate five out of the six H.O.T. A.P.E. flirting signs to the digital world, but we can all agree that there is no substitute for the only one that can be felt in the real world – touch!

7

First Dates . . .

When I carried out the New York part of my flirting research, I noticed an interesting phenomenon: the mating game there has a very particular pattern. There are set rules. The best illustration of this came in the form of a woman visiting from New York who joined one of my Fearless Flirting tours in London.

After showing people how to talk to strangers in everyday environments – the supermarket, gallery, book store – we ended the tour at a pub. She went up to the bar to order a drink. This woman was stunning, and she was the only one who didn't know it. As she stood at the bar waiting for her drink, she and the two men sitting there began a conversation. From afar, the English guys who were on the tour and I were watching, all smiles. 'She's doing great. Those guys are hanging on to her every word.' She came back a few minutes later with her drink. 'So,' I said, 'how did it go?' She looked a bit despondent. 'OK, I guess.' 'OK?!' we all said in incredulous unison. 'You seemed to be getting on well with those guys.' 'Not really. Neither of them asked for my number.' We all looked at each other. 'Why would they ask for your number? You had only been speaking with them for a brief time.'

And so she explained to the dumbfounded Englishmen how it worked in New York. She explained in great detail the exact protocol that is followed if someone likes you.

And this is her interpretation of how things went.

Step one: the initial meeting. You would meet and talk anywhere from ten minutes to an hour. If he was interested, he'd ask for your number, and if you were a 'modern' woman, you'd give it. If he didn't ask, then it was game over. Step two: the first date. Dinner if he was really interested; coffee or drinks were second best – that meant he wouldn't even spring for dinner. On the date, the woman would try to be interesting and charming but not too over the top. During the conversation, the woman would do most of the work, finding something to 'hook on to' to show how similar they were. But if a woman was really pretty, she would barely talk; she didn't have to do any work – he was lucky enough just to be sitting with her. It would end with a goodnight kiss.

Step three: the second date. This would definitely be at a restaurant. Hopefully in the same week. He would pay again. The idea for the woman would be to try to catch him and be everything he wants. She would kiss and make out a bit, but not much – she doesn't want to be slutty. Step four: on the third date, one of them would cook dinner and they would watch a movie, thereby creating a situation where they could have sex. If the woman were prudish, it could be the 'meet the friends' session instead, where one of you meets the other's group of friends.

At that point, she stopped. 'So, what happens after this?' I asked her. She said, 'I don't know; I never make it past the third date.'

Sounds exhausting. And while it might be nice to have a better idea of what is expected, this system doesn't leave much room for things to take a more organic course or even one where the woman has a more active role. This highly orchestrated approach isn't something I advocate. But, admittedly, without a strict dating protocol, the average flirter can feel slightly adrift. How should you handle things? Who should make the first move? How long to wait before getting in touch? What kind of date should it be? Where should you go?

If you're the person – regardless of gender – who is doing the asking, it can seem like you're constantly at risk of making a fool of yourself by contravening some unspecified law. And if you're being asked, every scenario can suddenly seem fraught with expectations that you're not sure you're going to meet. 'If he's taking me to a nice restaurant, will he expect me to know the superior vintages of Châteauneuf-du-Pape?'; 'If we go to a gig, is she expecting me to be able to sing all the lyrics to every song?'; 'If we're going to a movie, will he suddenly make a move over the popcorn? What if he gets butter on my new shirt?' It seems like potential pitfalls are lurking in every corner.

But I'd like you to consider a different, much more important, question: **what is the point of a date?** Is it to continue some ever-narrowing quest for The One? Is it to ensure that you and the person sitting opposite you become a couple? Is it to reassure yourself – and others – that you are Out There and doing your bit? Is it to have stories to tell your friends?

Actually, the primary goal of a date is none of these things. The goal of a date is simply **to build on your original attraction while having an enjoyable time**.

Let's remind ourselves of the Flirtology principles that have gotten you to this point:

- You have been approaching flirting as a mutually rewarding activity.
- You have embraced rejection and its magical filtering properties.
- You have considered your deal-breakers.
- You have gone for someone based on the rapport that your conversational approach sparked off.
- The very fact that you are on this date means that you already have an interest in each other and are open to finding out more.

In other words, you should be going on dates with the right people, not just anybody who asks. If this is the foundation, you can approach that first date with positivity: you have already worked out this is someone you can talk to, who matches most of your deal-breakers, and you have already scouted out some common ground. All you are doing now is taking that foundation and seeing if you can build on it.

Getting to a date

It may be that when you first met the other person, you set up a date with them immediately – a plan to see a certain film or go to a particular event. Good for you. I like the proactive approach. Or maybe you exchanged numbers and have taken it from there. This stage can be fun; as we've seen, the modern world is filled with a million ways for you to connect, and it can be a fantastic source of flirtatious frisson to be swapping amusing gifs or sending late-night texts.

But beware: don't let this phase go on too long. Entertaining as it might be to conduct an arm's-length dance of words through your phones, if you are looking for love you need to force yourselves out into the open. Wait too long in the phone zone, and you might find yourself caught in limbo there forever. It can simulate an intimacy that you just don't have. And, oddly, if this faux-intimacy gets too deep, it can make a real-life encounter awkward and disappointing as you both re-adjust to your actual personalities and the fact that you don't know each other as well as you thought.

So, use your phones to interact back and forth. Excellent entertainment, but you need to move it on. As we've seen in the previous chapter, set yourself a rule that works in your world. If you are still communicating remotely with no set date in sight after two weeks, no matter how fun this feels, force the issue. After getting revved up on a Fearless Flirting tour, one woman emailed me the next day to say the group went out to a bar afterwards. She met a guy and exchanged numbers. As she said in her email, 'We haven't set a date to meet up yet, but he is WhatsApping me like crazy!' Great in one way, but she wasn't sure it was going to go anywhere, and moving forward is what she was looking for.

And just in case I have been too subtle, ahem, either the woman or the man can do the asking out, just as anyone can make the approach. More people should do it. Another thing to be aware of is different communication styles. You might be happy to drop what you're doing at the hint of your phone's buzz, but your new friend might only check theirs a few times a day. They might be someone who likes to chat away on the phone, while you are allergic to speaking between the hours of nine to five. Be aware that other people's lives and communication styles won't necessarily match yours. And don't make assumptions about it. No, the reason she has taken over 48 hours to respond isn't necessarily because she isn't interested. It is actually because her grandmother is in hospital, and she has been with her family.

One client came to our session in a huff. She had met a guy the previous week. She originally thought he was nice, but later, after talking him over with a well-intentioned friend, they had decided he was rude. When I asked her why, it was because they had set a date for Saturday night, and here it was Thursday and she hadn't yet heard from him about where they were supposed to be meeting. Therefore, in her mind, he was inconsiderate, and she wasn't even sure that they were still on for the date. 'It's such a shame,' she lamented, 'he seemed like such a nice guy.'

This might seem extreme and, for the record, my client is a lovely person. But this is what happens when we are dealing with strangers and make assumptions about them. In her eyes, his behaviour seemed to mean that he wasn't making an effort for her. She kept a very organized diary and liked to have plans set out in advance. I pointed out that it was just as likely that he *was* interested but, having organized the initial time and date, he found it normal to wait until the day itself to firm up exact plans. Neither was wrong nor right; it was just a question of different styles. Make sure you are not imposing your own expectations on the other person.

Where to go?

If you are thinking about that first date, the first hurdle is what you should do on it. I have a two-sided rule for this: if you are doing the asking, **be decisive**. Nothing is less fun than a dithering conversation about whether to go for Chinese or Indian, or perhaps it would be fun to go to a movie instead. Your choice of venue doesn't have to be flashy, or expensive, or even highly inventive. (Although you could get a bit more creative than Nando's, apparently the most popular first-date location in Britain.) Great dates can be had without huge outlays of money. A walk in the park, bowling, brunch, art galleries. But whatever you come up with, make a decisive suggestion.

Conversely, if you are the one being asked, **be positive** and open-minded. Of course, you shouldn't feel coerced into doing something you'd hate – don't feel you have to go to a seafood restaurant if shellfish bring you out in hives – but be willing to try something new or go somewhere you haven't been before. If you really think you'll actively hate what's been suggested, counter it with something definite of your own. Don't put the other person on the spot and expect them to have a backup plan up their sleeve.

The best dates of all are the ones that build on the commonality you have already established: what was it that you were talking about with this person that got you so intrigued in the first place? Old records? Japanese anime? Off-road cycling? Then why not do an activity based around that? Remember the social contagion effect? If you're doing something together that they have positive feelings about, you will be encompassed in that bubble of happiness.

Remember, Flirtology is all about creating a life that is fulfilling *for you*. The date should be part of that continuum, not completely separate from it. It may sound obvious, but the best way to have a really good date is to **choose something you know you enjoy** doing. Don't choose things to impress, to be different or to show off what you can afford. This date is about presenting your authentic self, not a make-believe version of what you imagine the other person might prefer.

Consider what sort of venue and timing is most likely to create the best environment for you to get to know each other. One thing that can happen when people are in the throes of multiple dating – especially if they are on the digital dating scene – is that they can find themselves having a whole lot of one-hour coffee-shop-style dates. Essentially, you have to go on a date to work out whether you want to go on a date. The one-hour, low-investment time slot gives the sense of getting to know someone a bit better but without the appearance of having to risk much.

But you want to be on a date, not a job interview. Approaching dates like this gives the sense of wariness: you're not sure you want to invest much time in this person. But if you are worried that more than an hour with someone is likely to be too long, why are you meeting them at all? Remember, this is the point of having deal-breakers. You are not supposed to go on a date with everyone, just those who match your carefully considered criteria. And if you agree that they match your deal-breakers, then it is worth spending the time to get to know them. Flirtology is about maximizing opportunities and being efficient – this does not mean an endless parade of time-wasting dates that you fundamentally know are going nowhere.

 Who should pay?

This is a question that comes up with more and more frequency, and can often lead to an embarrassing moment at the end of an evening as you both fumble for your wallets and do the 'Let me.' 'No, let me' dance. Or, even worse, no one makes a move . . .

It used to be assumed that the man should pay, but, as we have already established, it also used to be accepted that it was a man's prerogative to do the asking out. Now that women are making almost as much money as men (don't get me started), it means they too have the choice to make the approach and to do the asking. Hooray. However, where things start to go wrong is when everyone still expects the man to pay.

The goal is to have anyone do the asking out, regardless of gender, with the expectation they will also do the paying. Not rolling in dough? No problem. A picnic or a walk should be affordable. The whole point of a date is to get to know someone better, to see if you want to do it again because you are interested in learning even more about them. No one said there was a minimum spend in all this.

What about splitting the bill? In my view, paying for someone is like giving them a present. One person gets to feel good because they have received a gift, and the other person gets to feel good because they have given a gift, resulting in two shiny people, both feeling special. This is why I prefer one person to pay instead of splitting the bill, where it becomes purely transactional. If you don't think you will be seeing the person again, or if the bill is quite high, splitting is probably fine. But to get around the whole 'who should pay' question, just take turns. One gets dinner, while the other gets drinks or says, 'I'll get it next time.' This way it's a constant flow of giving and receiving gifts. However, to avoid all of the initial awkwardness and fumbling, make it clear when you are asking that the date is your treat: 'I'd love to take you to . . .' If it goes well, they can always reciprocate next time.

Getting ready

You probably already have your rituals for getting ready: your favourite outfit, your 'date-night' aftershave, a bit of extra effort with your hair. And far be it from me to interfere with your tried-and-tested routines. But your sprucing up shouldn't just be about the physical; you also need to prepare your mind. That's right, you need **a suitable mental model**.

The purpose of having a mental model for a date is so that you don't let your mental chatter run away with you. Before a date, this mental chatter can work in two ways, often simultaneously. On the one hand, your brain propels itself into the future, with romantic notions of a wonderful courtship and perfect Instagram moments, hand in hand on a beach somewhere . . . And on the other hand, it can fall back into self-critical thinking: *'I'm terrible at dates; I'm sure to say something embarrassing. I always get nervous and talk too much'*, or *'I get all shy and don't say a word'*; *'What if he thinks I look like I'm trying too hard?'*; *'What if she thinks that I'm desperate?'*

Just stop! If a friend were saying any of the above, you would probably give them a stern shake and then invite them back to reality. But when it comes to our own mental chatter, we often let ourselves get carried away on the runaway train. Next stop: Never Neverland. I sometimes view my mental chatter as a whiny child who has just been denied ice-cream: best cut off quickly and indulged no further. At this stage, your date is neither your happily ever after nor judge and jury on your personality. You know you find them attractive, otherwise you wouldn't be here, but don't forget that they are a stranger minus one encounter. You don't really know much about them at all.

How to keep this voice quiet? It's worth recapping one of the first Flirtology lessons I taught you: **you are trying to attract people who like you for who you are**. That means you should be presenting your authentic self, not designing some act that you think will make them attracted to you. You are not trying to get on with everyone. That is a waste of time. If you act like yourself, you will attract people who like you. It's the perfect filtering mechanism. And this means that the mental chatter your brain is coming up with is irrelevant. You can't *make* someone like you, no matter what your mind has to say about it.

I was recently advising a guy in his thirties from Tasmania. His problem was not that he found it difficult to initiate flirting or even that he found it hard to convert these encounters into first dates. His problem was that he wasn't getting any second dates. Women always seemed to say that they'd had a really great time, that he was a nice guy, but that they didn't want to take it further. He was getting more and more worried about his dating technique. It was beginning to affect his confidence to the point where he had concluded that he just wasn't attractive. I talked to him about the kinds of conversations he was having, and at first I couldn't understand it either. He was clearly easy to talk to and had a good sense of humour. He seemed like a great guy. I then asked him if he was planning on leaving London at some point to go back to Tasmania. He said yes. I asked him if, on his dates with these English women, his return to Tasmania ever came up. 'Well, yes, I tell them that I will go back, but not for like at least five years!' And then I confirmed that he wasn't the problem at all. It wasn't his looks or personality that was off-putting, it was the idea of dating somebody who would one day move halfway around the world and they might have to leave their close friends and families and go with him!

What should he have done in this instance? Lie? Cover up his plans? Not exactly. It's bad manners to dupe people into going out with you under false pretences. But above all, he shouldn't have let it affect his confidence. There wasn't anything wrong with him. The right person, who was adventurous and wanted to travel, or who lived in the moment, would not be put off by his plans. Perhaps this was the perfect filtering mechanism for finding his Ms Right. Or maybe he should have been looking at dating fellow Antipodeans in London who, someday, would also be interested in moving back.

Remember some basic principles: first, **be open-minded** about the other person. As long as they meet your deal-breakers, then don't spend time before the date creating imaginary characteristics. Be ready to react to the other person for who they are, not on some preconceived notions you have formed about them based on one meeting and a few text messages. So, instead of: '*I think this could be The One. She seems absolutely perfect!*', try something more along the lines of: '*There was a real spark there when I last met her last time. I'm looking forward to finding out more.*'

Next, **don't look too far ahead**: keep your model grounded in the event itself. So, no hoping that you are about to meet the mother of your children or that this person is going to make up for all the guys who haven't worked out in the past. Keep it in the here and now. Much better to think '*I'm excited about tonight.*'

Stick to **what is under your control**, not what is dependent upon how the other person reacts. So, don't go for '*I'm hoping that I don't say something that will make him think I am weird.*' Instead, try something more along the lines of: '*It feels good to be attracted to someone. I hope I can build on that.*'

No matter how excited you are about this person, the same principles apply as when you first flirt with someone: small steps. You are about to be involved in one date together, approximately two hours of your lives. If it works well, it might lead to another. If the magic that you thought was there doesn't carry over into the first date, then it simply means that perhaps you are not a good match for each other. It is not a reflection on you as a person.

On the date

So, you've thought about your mental model and, I must admit, are lookin' good! (Hopefully, by now you can spot when someone is flirting with you?) You've organized tickets to the new tiny mirrors exhibition followed by dinner at a Vietnamese restaurant, as you've both already come clean about your prawn spring roll addiction. Admit it, you are looking forward to the night ahead. It's still natural to have a small hesitation as you step through the doors. But don't think of it as 'being nervous', think of it as 'frisson', the much sexier side of the same coin. You should be feeling a good buzz – full of hope, excitement and the air of the unexpected – not nervous trepidation. Understandably, you don't want to completely freeze up with nerves. And no, sorry, a shot of tequila is not the answer right now. The rules for overcoming this momentary hesitation are exactly the same as your earlier Flirtology lessons: remind yourself of your date mental model, make sure your body language is open, keep your head up, your arms uncrossed and smile. Remind yourself that your date is likely to have the same butterflies as you do!

You seem like a smart person, so you have undoubtedly been following my principles so far. Thus, there should be a good foundation for your flirtatious conversation to pick up where you left off. But it is natural for the different circumstances or first-date nerves to allow some self-consciousness to creep in. Don't worry. Remember what you have already learned:

- When you are feeling self-conscious, move your focus off yourself and on to the other person. Use participant observation to help reduce nerves.
- Use H.O.T. A.P.E. as a reminder of how to flirt and to show the other person you are interested. We like people who like us.
- Use the principles of commonality. This being your second encounter, you already have a basis to work on: you have a shared experience, possibly mutual acquaintances, and you should by now have established some areas of common interest. All fertile ground for asking a question that will ease you into the conversation. What got the conversation fired up when you last met them? Use that as a jumping-off point.
- Use props. The setting you are in – whether restaurant or bar or gig – should be full of conversation prompts. Failing that, one of my favourites is, 'What have you been up to since we last met?' It gives the other person space to talk about what they want, and it shows you are interested in hearing about their life.

Possible pitfalls

Energy flows where attention goes; this book is about focusing on the positive. However, if you find that you're getting a lot of first dates but not managing to take them further, there is a good possibility that you might be stumbling into these common pitfalls:

1. **Pitfall 1.** Are you giving the other person enough space in the conversation? Often, particularly when we are nervous, we tend to overcompensate by talking too much, by setting ourselves to transmit rather than receive. Are you allowing them space to answer? Or giving them the chance to ask you a question or take the lead in the conversation?

   If you think you are falling into this trap, then use participant observation to take a step back. Observe your behaviour. Are you really listening to the other person? A stream of nervous chatter is often due to fear of the dreaded uncomfortable silence. Don't always feel it is your responsibility to fill any silences. Contrary to popular thought, they are not akin to drowning in a teaspoon of water. Often, they are part of the ebb and flow of conversation, allowing for a change in direction.

2. **Pitfall 2.** Are you falling into the opposite trap and not giving enough of yourself? You can't both get to know each other if you are hiding who you are by moving into interviewer mode or not offering information about yourself. Mutual liking is created only when we give a little of

ourselves – the principle of reciprocity means that both people should be sharing and receiving equally.

If you think holding back about who you are might be your problem, ask yourself why? What are you afraid of? I am not talking about revealing all your darkest secrets on date one, but allow yourself to talk about things you enjoy, what you care about, what your ambitions are. Give your opinions, show your character.

3. **Pitfall 3.** Are you presenting some kind of facade, putting on an act based on what you think the other person will like? This is rarely convincing, and is also counterproductive. What is the point of trying to come across as someone you are not? You won't be able to keep it up indefinitely. I am getting tired just thinking about all that effort. And why are you assuming this person prefers the actor you to the real you?

We sometimes fall into this habit because we think the person we are with is somehow 'better' than us, that we need to impress them. If you sense this feeling of inferiority creeping over you, then check yourself. Arm yourself with a mental model to counteract these thoughts: 'I know that this person has things in common with me, otherwise we wouldn't be here.' Or, 'This isn't about whether they like me. This is about whether we like each other.'

4. **Pitfall 4.** Are you going back to your old checklists, judging everything that comes out of this person's mouth and mentally categorizing pros and cons? 'Doesn't like sushi, -1

point. Likes cuddly puppies, +1 point.' Relax. This isn't a game of Scrabble where you tally up the points at the end to determine if s/he is a winner. It's just a date.

If you have a tendency to do this, remember your deal-breakers. They are the only checklist you should care about – the five fundamental things that matter to you. Everything else is just noise.

5. **Pitfall 5.** And finally, while I don't generally advocate hard-and-fast rules about what to talk about, steer clear of discussing exes (if you are going to talk about influential people from the past, you might as well have a rousing discussion about Marie Curie) and avoid going into great detail about why you're single. How could that conversation ever turn out well?

The friend zone

There is one pitfall which deserves a discussion all to itself. And that is the dreaded 'friend zone', a no-man's-land that many men, in particular, find themselves relegated to after a date. To be clear – there is nothing wrong with mutually deciding that there's no romantic spark between you and if you see each other again it will simply be as friends. But note the 'mutual' in that sentence. The friend zone is something different. It's where one of you is still interested in a romantic sense, but the other person consigns them to a different category: pals. Why is this, and what can we do about it?

One of the major reasons people get put in the friend zone is because they have put themselves there already. It's where they are when they show up; the other person simply follows their lead. What do you expect is going to happen when you put yourself in the role of agony aunt and advice-giver? One of my male clients reported back after a first date. His date's comment afterwards was that she 'didn't think there was much chemistry, but thank you for such great career advice'. They aren't going to see each other again, but she is now going to quit her job and retrain. Sexy stuff.

What it boils down to is that if you are not to be classified as 'the friend', the other person has to think they would like to get naked with you at some point. There needs to be a sexual undertone in the air. Otherwise, invite them to your bridge group, because the only place you'll be getting any action is at the card table. Another male client came to me with the same problem – he felt he was living in the friend zone whenever he tried to get close to anyone. I asked him, 'What is flirting to you?' He responded that it was about having a friendly chat, where two people can find if they share more in common. Friendly chat! Now this is an interesting conundrum. As you know, the Flirtology approach is a gentle, step-by-step process. And, yes, commonality is an important principle. But there's more to it than that. When we are looking to **flirt with intent**, there is an extra ingredient. Remember H.O.T. A.P.E.? If you are deploying all the weapons at your disposal, then everything from your body language to your eye contact to the way you have subtly brushed their hand with yours should be telling them that this interaction is about more than your shared love of West End musicals.

But this is the exact place where many people falter. It seems that the element of showing one's sexuality is the reason people might wander into the friend zone; they feel that being rejected as a potential friend would hurt less than being rejected as a potential romantic partner. Therefore, as way of protection, they put their feet up, make a nice cuppa and turn into expert advice-giver.

If being a friend, a confidante, is a role that you are used to, it's very easy to slip into it, especially if you are already feeling a bit nervous to begin with. It's like an old, soft jumper: comfy and reliable. Talking to someone about their problems, or about bland, easy subjects, can fill the space on the date. But it makes the other person think of their loyal dog rather than making them think about what is Under That Jumper. And this sexual undertone is the main differentiator between a potential new friend and a potential new boy/girlfriend. New friends are always nice to have, but most people tell me they are not looking for a new friend; they are looking for a romantic partner.

Be really honest. Do you recognize yourself in this? And, if so, is there anything you can do about it? Yes. You can create chemistry yourself. What most people don't realize is that chemistry can be manufactured through our actions and behaviours. This idea might contradict every 'love at first sight' romantic story, but it is true. Chemistry doesn't always just appear magically. There are things that we can do to create more chemistry. As we have previously discussed, touch and laughter both spark physiological responses in the body, stimulating the reward centre of the brain, resulting in pleasurable feelings. But science has also shown that participating in thrilling activities, such as riding roller coasters and watching scary movies, heighten arousal levels, which can increase physical attraction. As if you needed another reason to watch *Scream Master Part 17* on your date?! One consequence of sharing new and arousing activities with another person is increased relationship quality.

If you recall, I have already pointed out that chemistry alone is not a good indication of who will be a good match with you. That is what the deal-breakers are for. And part of the reason for this is that 'chemistry' between two people is not an absolute state. It is subject to ebb and flow. And, contrary to how it's been presented to us, chemistry is not something that hits you on first meeting someone or never materializes at all. So, at least wait until you've spent some time doing chemistry-inducing things – days on roller coasters and nights laughing and holding hands at a comedy show – before making a snap judgement on chemistry levels.

People are often friend-zoned because the other person isn't feeling the chemistry. But whether or not you are put in the friend category is really about how you feel about yourself and then how you portray this to others. Act like a friend, you will be regarded as one. Act like a potential lover and you will be seen as one. And although there are practical tools that can help you 'fake it till you make it', it really starts from inside of you. Are you accessing the flirty, or even sexual, part of yourself? No? Well then, how can you expect someone else to? In order for others to see something in us, we must first be able to see it in ourselves. As we saw in Chapter 2, our attractiveness lies to a great extent in our own confidence. This isn't to do with rating ourselves on some imaginary scale. It is to do with ensuring that we are feeling at our best – wearing clothes that make us feel attractive, being in a place that makes us feel we can be ourselves. Accessing the flirtatious side of our personalities means that we are showing up from the right place, and that place comes from inside of us. The mental model is '*I'm feeling good tonight.*'

If you happen to be someone who never fancies anyone, it could be the same issue – you haven't accessed that flirty place inside yourself. You need to first find this part of yourself before you can find it in others. I remember my brother would get frustrated with me when we were younger. 'Your friend Joe was totally flirting with me!' He would roll his eyes, 'You think *everyone* is flirting with you!' He was right, I did. It was because I was always flirting with everyone. We view the world the way we relate to the world. I had accessed my inner flirt and could see it in others as well. As a bonus, it was really fun annoying my brother.

What is your intent when you are on a date with someone you like? H.O.T. A.P.E. helps us display outward signs of attraction: you can touch the person's hand, use extended eye contact, stand closer, etc. But this feeling, this intent, starts from the inside. How you are feeling? Flirty? Sexy? Attractive? If you are feeling this way, you don't even have to think about what exact moves to make; they will come naturally. The outside behaviours will happen in relation to your inside feelings. You won't even have to use precious brain cells thinking about it. You can divert all your attention to the amazing flirting encounter that is unfolding right in front of you.

What if it's not working out?

We've all been there. You're on a date with someone, and no matter how much you initially thought that they might be a good match, it's becoming clear that they're not the right person for you. As I've said before, I believe that if someone meets your dealbreakers, you should give them three dates to see if you are a good match. But what if you realize that even having all of your dealbreakers can't counteract the fact that their laugh reminds you of a fire siren? The effect keeps making you drift off, debating what you would save if your house caught on fire . . . The hour stretching in front of you is looking longer with every passing minute, and your greatest fear is that they might actually want to meet up again.

If you happen to find yourself in this position, it is fine to admit to yourself that this isn't going to be your happily ever after. But **ask yourself if there is anything that you can do differently**. Are you just sitting back in judgement while they ramble on about their Z-list celebrity sightings without trying to change the conversation to a subject you are both interested in? If you are finding them monosyllabic, is it because you are taking up the entire conversation and not giving them room to contribute? Or if you are feeling they are taking up too much air time and not asking you anything about yourself, could it be because you are in interview mode, asking a question and then sitting back and listening to the long monologue? Of course we sometimes find people not to our taste. But we can try to take some ownership of the dynamic. Switch it up. Start offering some information about yourself, your interests and passions. Take charge of the conversation a bit more. If it's not working, change something you are doing, don't just withdraw from the other person.

Just because you have already decided that you will probably never see this person again, **it doesn't mean that nothing good can come out of the interaction.** Perhaps this is your chance to learn about the fascinating world of birds of prey or an opportunity to hear the opposing side of an issue. These days we only surround ourselves with like-minded people. This could be an interesting exercise in being exposed to diversity.

At this point, it's clear that this person won't be your future partner. However, **on a human to human level, could you spare an hour or so to finish the date?** I am not a fan of doing anything out of politeness. I think that when our behaviour is governed by what is expected of us, it often comes at the expense of being true to ourselves. However, I am a big fan of us being kind to each other. So, in this spirit of kindness, can you relate to this person in a different way, find whatever pleasure there is in their company and finish the date?

But, **if you have gone through the first three points and it still feels excruciating, then make your exit.** Because the number one rule of Flirtology is to be true to yourself. In this case, you simply say, 'Thank you for taking the time to meet me, but unfortunately I have to go now. Enjoy the rest of your day.' (Or something to this effect.) And then you leave . . . There is no need to feel guilty. You have done everything that you can possibly do.

What you don't want to do is what my friend did. We met up for coffee one afternoon, and she looked like something that the cat had dragged in: hungover, tired and, if I must say, a bit grumpy. She told me that she'd had a terrible date the night before. 'Where did you go?' I asked. 'Well, we started off in a restaurant, then we went on to a bar, and then we went to a club. I got home at about 3 a.m.' 'Why on earth did you stay so long?' I asked her. 'Well, there just never seemed a good time to bail out.' Instead, she had let herself drift into the next part of the date, and the next, and the next. I asked her, 'At what point did you know that he wasn't for you?' 'Oh, probably after the first course.'

Avoid this mistake. Don't say yes to those things that extend the date. All it takes to make a graceful exit is a simple phrase or two: 'It was nice meeting you, but I am afraid I have something else to do/have an early start tomorrow/am feeling tired.'

Look, letting someone down is never going to be the most fun you've ever had, and there is no exact script to follow. But the bottom line is that you still have to be true to yourself while considering someone else's feelings. Being fuzzy in your intention towards them does not make you a nicer person or the let-down easier for them; it just makes them more confused. The kindest thing you can do is be clear with them that it's not going to work, but there's no need to announce at the end of proceedings, 'Nope, we won't ever be seeing each other again. Lose my number, please!' My advice is to end the date on a friendly but non-committal note. If they put you on the spot or ask you straight out about seeing them again, be honest. Otherwise, the next morning send a message saying something like, 'Thanks for your time last night, but I just don't think it is going to work out.' Don't get dragged into reasons why; just be clear and simple about it. And, above all, don't say that you 'didn't feel any chemistry'. For some reason, people believe this is a nice way to do it. Trust me, it isn't. We've got half of the single population walking around thinking they have as much sexual appeal as a wet mop because of this 'nice' text send-off.

What if it *is* working out?

At the other end of the spectrum is the etiquette of what to do if things are going very, very well indeed. Let us be frank: is it OK to sleep with someone on your first date? Well, when I asked this question of my New York informant from the beginning of the chapter, she made it clear that you would only have sex with someone if you had no long-term interest in them. They could be a quick interlude because you found them hot, or needed to 'to take the edge off' while you played nicely, waiting for the guy who you think might be a long-term prospect. But when I conducted my flirting research in London, both men and women said that they had been involved in long-term relationships that had sprung from first-date sex. Apparently, most men in London don't necessarily think that you are the Wrong Sort of Girl if you consent to get naked with them too early. As one said, 'There had to be something that got us into bed in the first place. Why wouldn't you see if there was more to explore?'

What this dichotomy illustrates is that the answer to the question 'Is it OK?' is dependent on a host of factors. Different cultures, different religions, different traditions, different social strata, different peer groups all have an opinion on the matter. Whether it's acknowledged or not, most of these opinions revolve around who has ownership of a woman's sexuality. This is a huge area, one where women often don't have a public voice. My own research in different countries had already piqued my interest in this subject, and that interest has since been expanded by reading some groundbreaking studies on sexuality, conducted by female sexologists, in the book *What Do Women Want? Adventures in the Science of Female Desire* by Daniel Bergner. This has made me consider two important factors: how far societal expectations affect women's sexuality, and also how until quite recently it has been men who have led the study of sex and sexual activity. Is it any wonder that women's voices haven't been clearly heard?

The prevalence of one-night stands is directly related to whether or not a woman feels she will be negatively perceived for her actions. As I saw in my own research, in Stockholm, a place with one of the highest gender equality levels in the world, the response from both men and women was that Swedish women were free to do what they wanted. They had just as much right to have sex without stigma as the men. As one sensible Swedish male said, 'Swedish men are not stupid. If we judged women for it, we would get less of it.'

Although it's hard to strip away all of these influences and expectations that might revolve around one-night stands, the most important opinion on what to do is your own. This is a point where you have to make up your own mind.

What I would say is the following: if you are feeling the vibe after a fabulous first date, consider why you want to do it. If you think it will give you validation, or you are doing it as a way to get attention, or you feel you 'owe' someone something, then these are not good reasons to have sex! However, if it's purely because the sparks are flying and H.O.T. A.P.E. has inspired some hot action, well, then, you're an adult. Why not?

Let go of the notion that having sex early on puts you on some different track to a long-lasting relationship. And if someone is using this in judgement against you, best to get rid of them now. As always, do what feels right for you and you will automatically filter out anyone who is not a good match. Isn't this way so much better?

Looking ahead

What's the best possible first date? Simple: one that makes you both want to go on a second one. By now, you don't need me to tell you how that's done. If your date is going brilliantly, if you're reading the signs right, if both you and the other person are in the zone, then do this simple trick: ask for a second one.

8

. . . and beyond

WE ARE NEARING the end, you and I. I hope by now you realize that I think you are fabulous. I would like nothing better than to imagine you finding that perfect somebody and having a wondrous time together. And I hope I have equipped you not only to find the person you are looking for but to enjoy the process while you do it. Not every flirting encounter will lead to a date; not every date will lead to a relationship, but each encounter holds the seed of possibility and improves the way we interact with the world.

My firm belief is that Flirtology is an aid to life whether you are in a relationship or not. So, I would like to leave you some principles to help you on your way – whether you have found love the Flirtology way or whether you are still looking.

In the early throes of a relationship, high on the giddiness that a new romance can bring to our lives, we can find ourselves losing ourselves in love. There is much in this feeling to savour. And I wouldn't want to prevent you from revelling in the high that love can engender. But please bear some things in mind:

1. Be open to the adventure that a new relationship can bring. But also be aware that this person is there to complement your life, not to fill holes in it for you. As well as sharing this new terrain with a new partner, continue to do things that are right for you, to make sure that your life is as complete and fulfilled as possible.

2. Bring your interests to the party too. Remember you found each other because you were a good match. Because you looked for this person the Flirtology way, they were attracted to you for who you are. Don't lose sight of yourself just because there is a new someone in your life.

3. A relationship is not a 'goal'; it is a new shared domain to explore with someone else. Just because you have found someone does not mean you should let the tenets of Flirtology disappear from your life. I want to be able to imagine you greeting every occasion – in work, in leisure, in general life – with a Flirtology-inspired attitude, which includes:

   • a positive mental model
   • making the most of every opportunity
   • body language that is approachable and open

- a willingness to interact with everyone, whilst still holding firmly to your personal boundaries
- fully embracing that you are responsible for your own well-being.

Armed with these principles, everything from a networking event to a morning run is an opportunity to make life a little more positive for both you and the people around you. And this can only enrich any relationship you are in.

For those of you who are still continuing the search, the message I want to leave you with is that you should be enjoying every step of the journey. If you are not, then it's time to step back and re-evaluate, because that is not the Flirtology way. Flirtology is about recognizing what you do have rather than bemoaning what you don't.

And remember one of the most important principles of all: **you should be doing the things that make you happy**. Nothing is more important than your personal well-being. Nothing. For without this, you are of no good to anyone. Examine your life in this light: are you doing things that are right for you right now, or are you burying yourself under the expectations of others?

We are currently living our lives in a rigid structure of expectation: perfect partner, perfect children, perfect looks and perfect bank balance. It's the story we have been sold by society, and it is often reinforced by well-meaning family and friends. (They can't help it; they are living in the same structure that we are.) We rarely pause to question this story and ask if it's what *we* want. Take, for example, a CEO friend of mine who comes from a traditional family background. She confided in me that she was so tired of her family pressuring her to find a husband. 'I have an MBA from a top university, I run a successful company, I am now working on my law degree, but yet I am still looked at as a failure because I don't have a husband.' She has decided to 'stop wasting time chasing guys' and, with this extra time, has turned to yoga. She absolutely glows when she talks about her new-found love.

In my own story, my participation in the structure involved constantly pressuring myself about my weight. You might relate. Never satisfied, always wanting to lose 'just five more pounds', until one day it dawned on me that I was living according to rules that I didn't even believe in. It's so ingrained, so deeply entrenched, that it's very hard to notice at first. But I began questioning why. And then I could see that not only was this constant pressure to conform causing me much angst and pain but that it wasn't even real. Where did this idea even come from? So, I thought, 'This is ridiculous. This makes no sense. I am going to stop now.' And I stepped outside of the structure as well.

We are also told that the first route to happiness is being in love, finding that one person for a lifelong relationship. But, actually, if it's any old relationship you are after, assuming you have good hygiene habits and don't leave your underwear strewn across the floor, it's not really hard to find *someone* to be in a relationship with. Often, people will grab on to whomever is around, hoping that being in a relationship with someone, anyone, will be better than not being in one at all. We have all made this mistake and have found it not to be the case. But here is what you are not told: it's not the act of being in *any* relationship that brings happiness but being in a healthy, loving and equal partnership.

Flirtology is about finding the *right* match, not any match. This is what I want for you, my Flirtology compadres: a relationship that allows you to be yourself, one where you feel equal and valued, and one where you can express every side of your personality. Remember when you were figuring out your deal-breakers? You weren't looking for a particular physical type or creating a lengthy list of perfect check-box attributes. By first looking inwards, you were figuring out what qualities in another person were vitally important to you. And I want you to find someone who fulfils these qualities.

But your happiness revolves around more than achieving 'the relationship'. It is my belief that, as wonderful as love relationships can be, they are not the only thing you need. Happiness comes not in the form of one relationship but in many quality relationships: workmates, dear friends, neighbours, family members, community. I want to think of you improving relationships on every level, from relationships with your brothers to relationships with the woman at the checkout counter. They are all important and bring happiness to both you and the other party.

However, we can only do this if we step out into the world and interact with people – especially with people who might at first appear different to us. I love living in a diverse city like London. Sometimes I purposely try to talk to someone whom I normally wouldn't come into contact with in my day-to-day life. I am never disappointed. Sometimes the exchanges are short and perfunctory, which is fine; sometimes they are warm and lengthy. I once met my 'twin', who came in the form of a 50-year-old Korean man, whilst standing in front of a bakery window on a rainy night in London. The more we spoke, the more we realized that we had a lot in common, despite our obvious external differences. After a nice chat, and a chicken recipe exchange, we gave each other a high-five and walked off in separate directions into the night. I like connecting with strangers for moments in time. I like being reminded that most people are just like me: doing the best they can and just trying to have a good life. But I find that the tendency of technological progress is to make opportunities for these inter-actions more rare.

My husband and I used to go to spin class together. Somehow, the pain lessened when I could make snarky comments to him whilst we were trudging up an imaginary hill. We recently went again, but this time the bikes had been upgraded to the highest technology. And instead of us all grooving together to our instruc-tor's latest favourite song, we all wore headsets through which we would hear the music separately along with our instructor's instructions. It was less about us all experiencing the class together and more about us being in the same room cycling. As for me being able to unburden my pain on to my husband, he just didn't seem delighted to remove his headphones every time I wanted to complain. (Perhaps he sees this technological advancement as an improvement!) Yes, there were screens and zones and lots of fancy gadgets, but we were more isolated. I think this has become a very common trend. The more technologically advanced society becomes, the further apart we are being pulled. The more con-venient things become, the less interaction we have with each other. No need to ask a friendly stranger for directions, you have Google maps. The last frontier of interacting with strangers was deciding who you would ask to take a photo of you. You had to carefully scan people as they walked by: who didn't look too busy, who was most likely not to run off with your camera. At last you would make your selection and the chosen person would recognize the honour and happily comply. This is now gone. What has taken its place? The selfie stick.

Yes, our digital world has helped us enormously. We are able to communicate so freely. With a mere tap, I can communicate with my family and friends from around the world. On top of that we can plot our journeys, see how many steps we've taken, check the weather and even use our phones as an alarm clock so that they are the first thing we see when we wake up, thus ensuring that the love story begins again each day.

For myself, I recognized that whilst I am grateful for many things about it, I don't want a love story with my phone. Nor do I want to start my day with it. So, I moved my phone out of the bedroom and bought a clock radio instead. I now wake up to my favourite radio station, and all urges to 'quickly check something' in the middle of the night have been eliminated. I have deleted all social-media apps from my phone, though they still remain on my desktop. I was aware that I was using them so I wouldn't have to deal with any feelings of boredom, and I didn't like that; we need to be bored sometimes. It wasn't just because of the distraction factor that I have cut back on my social-media participation. It was also because I realized that, without even meaning to, all the pictures I posted were of an idealized life: countless holidays with my husband or friends from around the world, featuring amazing meals and beautiful sunsets. Fun. Fun. Fun! But I wasn't posting the innocuous daily occurrences that make up most of my life: me in front of the computer, me emptying the dishwasher, me preparing dinner. I was only showing one constructed version of my life, and I didn't like it. Not only was this a distortion of the truth, but I was visually ticking off the expected boxes of 'happiness' rather than representing myself in my own individual way. I don't want to do this any more.

I think these changes are worth it, because if our attention is always focused online, it means that we are not engaging with each other in the real world. How can we have a talk about pastries with Korean men if we are looking down all the time?

I firmly believe that happiness lies not in checking the milestones of life off on a pre-ordered route and displaying them to the world, but in listening to your inner voice, finding your own path. Flirtology is a way to help you navigate your own journey.

An illustration of this came to me recently from the other side of the world. I am a frequent speaker in the Far East. As far as one can generalize about such a diverse and varied set of countries, great changes are afoot there and the pan-Asian countries feel dynamic and exciting. The last time I was there, I met Ayesha. Ayesha is Malaysian. She is the president of a big company; she is smart, funny, enthusiastic and 42. She desperately wanted to find a partner so she could have a child. The model she was expected to follow was to find a man slightly older than herself who would 'take care' of her. She pursued this goal, as she did everything else, with 100 per cent effort. She joined groups, was the founder of Meetups, signed up for hobbies, went to every party she was asked to join. When she came to me for private coaching, I asked her if at this point in her life she was more interested in the partner or the child. She replied, 'The child.' And this realization made her change tack from the conventional path; while she couldn't make a wonderful partner magically appear, she could do something about her desire to have a child. She decided to try on her own. As an economically independent woman, she could outsource things, which meant she could work and have a child. And in deciding this, she also realized that when it came to men, she needn't look for the type of man that would have been the prize partner in previous generations. With her own economic success, there was no need to be reliant on anyone else's.

A month later, she contacted me and said she had met a 28-year-old man on her diving trip, and they had been spending loads of time together. She was wary about the age difference but said they were having a lot of fun. She mentioned a few minor issues that had come up because of the age question. I assured her there were always minor issues that come up in relationships, regardless of age. Five months later, I met her in London. She was glowing. She was in love. Last month she sent me a message telling me that she was pregnant with his child. They were both incredibly happy.

Why do I tell you this (apart from as a lovely story with a happy ending)? I tell you because, happy-ever-after as her story might be, the route she took to get there was not the traditional one she was expected to follow. She stepped outside of the structure to find a way that better suited her. Traditionally, a woman waits for a partner before she has a child. But Ayesha made the decision to do what she really wanted without being dependent on other people. Traditionally, society told her that she should have been looking for a slightly older man who would provide for her. But when she really looked at herself, she realized this was not what she needed. She was willing to open up her horizons, to turn the expectations of society upside down and to embrace a new social dynamic. She changed her perspective on a partner search, and she made her own choices.

I want you to take this approach to your own lives. Step away from preconceived rules, step away from the expectations. Think about **what really matters to you** and how to achieve it your way. Not in the way that you have been told to in books and movies, not in the way your friends or family have done before, but in the way that works for the person that you are. This holds true regardless of your gender or whether you are on the flirt scene in London, New York or anywhere in the world. Make connections, take hold of your own story and allow yourself to write your own happy ending. It all starts with just one question.

So, who are you going to talk to today?

Notes

4   '**There are 91 million people . . .**'

According to a new report from GlobalWebIndex, there are more than 91 million people around the world using dating apps, and two-thirds of these users are men.

https://www.theguardian.com/technology/2015/feb/17/mobile-dating-apps-tinder-two-thirds-men

4   '**According to Pew, a leading think tank . . .**'

http://www.pewresearch.org/topics/online-dating/

4   '**But the number of Americans who are in a marriage . . .**'

http://www.pewresearch.org/topics/online-dating/

4   '**88 per cent met their partner offline . . .**'

http://www.pewresearch.org/topics/online-dating/

4   '**In the UK, 15 million singles . . .**'

There are surprisingly few stats about online dating in the UK. Unlike the Pew Research Center in the US, an impartial think tank, most stats in the UK come from the dating agencies themselves. I found this figure from the link below.

https://visual.ly/community/infographic/love-and-sex/uk-online-dating-stats-dating-friends

The source below claims there are 20 million people in the UK using online dating every month. Again, the stats come from a different UK online dating agency.
http://www.cosmopolitan.com/uk/love-sex/relationships/a27169/infographic-on-dating-in-the-uk-mysinglefriend/

4   **'But a study surveying 18–35-year-olds . . .'**
A study of 2,300 people between 18 and 35 years old reveals that 39 per cent met through friends, 22 per cent social situations, 18 per cent work, 10 per cent online dating, 6 per cent social media.
https://www.maturitydating.co.uk/increased-use-online-dating/

4   **'Its estimated worth is more than £2 billion globally . . .'**
http://www.huffingtonpost.co.uk/2012/10/26/the-2bn-relationship-the-business-of-online-dating_n_2024458.html

5   **'In a study of Americans, only 20 per cent . . .'**
http://marketing-assets.avvo.com/media-resources/avvo-research/2016/avvo_relationship_study_2016_final_report.pdf

5   **'But the average internet dater spends . . .'**
Motivated by the lack of research into the area of online dating and by frustration in dealing with the non-transparency of the dating agencies, these social scientists decided to undertake the largest and most comprehensive study in this field to date.
Finkel, E. J. et al., 'Online Dating: A Critical Analysis From the Perspective of Psychological Science', *Association for Psychological Science*, vol. 13, no. 1, 2012, pp. 3–66.

5   **'Thirty-three per cent of online daters . . .'**
https://www.datingsitesreviews.com/article.php?story=5-facts-about-online-dating-from-pew-research-center

6   **'The UN predicts that by 2050 . . .'**
http://www.un.org/en/development/desa/population/publications/pdf/popfacts/PopFacts_2014-3.pdf

6   **'Numerous studies show us . . .'**
Yao, M. and Z. Zhong, 'Loneliness, Social Contacts and Internet Addiction: A Cross-Lagged Panel Study', *Computers in Human Behavior*, January 2014, pp. 164–170.

6   **'To make things worse . . .'**
'Discussion networks are smaller in 2004 than in 1985. The number of people saying there is no one with whom they discuss important matters nearly tripled. The mean network size decreases by about a third (one confidant), from 2.94 in 1985 to 2.08 in 2004. The modal respondent now reports having no confidant; the modal respondent in 1985 had three confidants.'
McPherson, J. M. and L. Smith-Lovin and M. Brashears, 'Social Isolation in America: Changes in Core Discussion Networks over Two Decades', *American Sociological Review*, vol. 71, no. 3, June 2006, pp. 353–75.

6   **'One study concludes that the digital world . . .'**
Yao, M. and Z. Zhong, 'Loneliness, Social Contacts and Internet Addiction: A Cross-Lagged Panel Study', *Computers in Human Behavior*, January 2014.

7   **'As the psychologist Adam Alter . . .'**
https://www.ted.com/talks/adam_alter_why_our_screens_make_us_less_happy

7   **'According to a British study . . .'**
This number actually may be too low, since people tend to underestimate their own mobile usage. In a 2015 Gallup survey, 61 per cent of people said they checked their phones less frequently than others they knew.
http://www.tecmark.co.uk/smartphone-usage-data-uk-2014/

7   **'In a 2015 Pew Survey . . .'**
This statistic was referenced in a *New York Review of Books* article surrounding how the digital age has influenced our communication styles.
http://www.nybooks.com/articles/2016/02/25/we-are-hopelessly-hooked/
The orginial Pew study:
http://www.pewinternet.org/2015/04/01/us-smartphone-use-in-2015/

8   'In fact, the very *presence* . . .'
Przybylski, A. K. and N. Weinstein, 'Can You Connect With Me Now? How the Presence of Mobile Communication Technology Influences Face-to-Face Conversation Quality', *Journal of Social and Personal Relationships*, vol. 30, no. 3, July 2012, pp. 237–46.

41 'A power dynamic between the sexes . . .'
Mark Dyble, an anthropologist at University College London, puts it: 'There is still this wider perception that hunter-gatherers are more macho or male-dominated. We'd argue it was only with the emergence of agriculture, when people could start to accumulate resources, that inequality emerged.'
https://www.theguardian.com/science/2015/may/14/early-men-women-equal-scientists

41 'In India, "The archaeological evidence . . .'
Singh, K. S., 'Gender roles in history: women as hunters', *Gender, Technology and Development*, vol. 5, no. 1, 2001, pp. 113–24.

41 'To take one modern-day example . . .'
In the Philippines, the Aeta women hunt in groups and with dogs, and have a 31 per cent success rate as opposed to 17 per cent for men. Their rates are even better when they combine forces with men: mixed hunting groups have a full 41 per cent success rate among the Aeta.
Estioko-Griffin, A. and P. Bion Griffin, 'Woman the Hunter: The Agta', in F. Dahlberg (ed.), *Woman the Gatherer*, New Haven, CT, Yale University Press, 1983, p. 120.

41 'There are plenty of . . .'
Sahlins, M., 'The Original Affluent Society' in *The Politics of Egalitarianism: Theory and Practice*, ed. J. Solway, New York, Berghahn Books, 2006, pp. 79–98.

41 '. . . or animism as our main . . .'
https://link.springer.com/article/10.1007/s12110-016-9260-0#Fig2

42 'Chimpanzees are said to be . . .'
Hecht, Jeff, 'Chimps are Human, Gene Study Implies', *New Scientist*, May 2003. https://www.newscientist.com/article/dn3744-chimps-are-human-gene-study-implies/

42 **'Promiscuity is encouraged . . .'**
Manson, J. H. et al., 'Nonconceptive Sexual Behavior in Bonobos and Capuchins', *International Journal of Primatology*, vol. 18, no. 5, 1997, pp. 767–86.

42 **'Well, unlike the case of the chimps . . .'**
Angier, Natalie, 'Beware the Bonds of Female Bonobos', *New York Times*, 10 September 2016.

44 **'It is not a coincidence that in Sweden . . .'**
http://reports.weforum.org/global-gender-gap-report-2015/the-global-gender-gap-index-results-in-2015/

63 **'Negative experiences tend to stand out to us . . .'**
https://www.psychologytoday.com/articles/200306/our-brains-negative-bias

64 **'I was recently reading an article in *The Economist* . . .'**
https://www.economist.com/news/asia/21706321-most-japanese-want-be-married-are-finding-it-hard-i-dont

65 **'Some rather off-putting online dating stats . . .'**
http://www.statisticbrain.com/online-dating-statistics/

80 **'What percentage of our weight is determined by genes? . . .'**
Mann, T., *Secrets from the Eating Lab*, New York, Harper Wave, 2015.

118 **'My own research, backed up by other studies . . .'**
Kellerman, J., 'Looking and Loving: The Effects of Mutual Gaze on Feelings of Romantic Love', *The Journal of Research in Personality*, vol. 23, no. 2, June 1989, pp. 145–61.
And, second source: http://www.sirc.org/publik/flirt.html

119 **'It not only gives a positive impression . . .'**
Mobbs, Dean et al., 'Humor Modulates the Mesolimbic Reward Centers', *Neuron*, vol. 40, no. 5, 4 December 2003, pp. 1041–8.

124 **'Even if you're in a supermarket . . .'**
https://www.theguardian.com/commentisfree/2016/aug/12/hispsters-handle-unpalatable-truth-avocado-toast

125 'Psychologists refer to this as social contagion . . .'
Hsee, C. K. et al., 'Assessments of the Emotional States of Others – Conscious Judgements Versus Emotional Contagion', *Journal of Social and Clinical Psychology*, vol. 11, no. 2, 1992, pp. 119–28.

145 'In one experiment, couples who engaged . . .'
Holt-Lunstad, J. et al., 'Influence of a "Warm Touch" Support Enhancement Intervention Among Married Couples on Ambulatory Blood Pressure, Oxytocin, Alpha Amylase, and Cortisol', *Psychosomatic Medicine*, vol. 70, no. 9, 2008, pp. 976–85.

147 'The scientists, led by Dr Ivanka Savic . . .'
Savic, I., 'Pheromone Processing in Relation to Sex and Sexual Orientation', in C. Mucignat-Caretta (ed.), *Neurobiology of Chemical Communication*, Boca Raton, CRC Press/Taylor & Francis, 2014.

173 'Studies have shown that . . .'
Yao, M. and Z. Zhong, 'Loneliness, Social Contacts and Internet Addiction: A Cross-Lagged Panel Study', *Computers in Human Behavior*, January 2014.

173 'The psychologist Adam Alter . . .'
https://www.ted.com/talks/adam_alter_why_our_screens_make_us_less_happy

186 'It won't surprise you . . .'
Zajonc, R. B., 'Attitudinal Effects of Mere Exposure', *Journal of Personality and Social Psychology*, vol. 9, no. 2, June 1968, pp. 1–27.

187 'Research by Bob Zajonc . . .'
Zajonc, R. B., 'Attitudinal Effects of Mere Exposure', *Journal of Personality and Social Psychology*, vol. 9, no. 2, June 1968, pp. 1–27.

188 'That is, they evaluated the woman . . .'
Moreland, R. and S. Beach, 'Exposure Effects in the Classroom: The Development of Affinity Among Students', *Journal of Experimental Social Psychology*, vol. 28, no. 3, May 1992, pp. 255–76.

189 'In fact, most college friendships . . .'
Festinger, L. and S. Schachter, and K. Back, *Social Pressures in Informal Groups: A Study of Human Factors in Housing*, Palo Alto, California, Stanford University Press, 1950.

192 'Roughly half of all relationships . . .'
Parks, M. R., *Personal Relationships and Personal Networks*, Mahwah, NJ, Lawrence Erlbaum Associates, 2007.

215 'But science has also shown . . .'
Dutton, D. G. and A. P. Aron, 'Some Evidence for Heightened Sexual Attraction Under Conditions of High Anxiety', *Journal of Personality and Social Psychology*, vol. 30, no. 4, 1974, pp. 510–17.

216 'As if you needed another . . .'
Aron, A. et al., 'Couples' Shared Participation in Novel and Arousing Activities and Experienced Relationship Quality', *Journal of Personality and Social Psychology*, vol. 78, no. 2, 2000, pp. 273–84.

About the Author

Jean Smith is the world's leading authority on flirting. She has degrees in both social and cultural anthropology and has researched flirting behaviour in a variety of countries.

Jean is a regular contributor to the media and has appeared on television and radio (including *BBC Breakfast*, *GMTV*, *This Morning*, *Woman's Hour* and *Daybreak*). She has also featured in a wide variety of newspapers and magazines, including *Marie Claire*, *Psychologies*, *The Times* and the *Daily Telegraph* as well as regularly appearing in the international press. Jean's TEDx talk on the science of flirting has attracted over two million views.

She is the founder of Flirtology and lives in London.

To find out more about Jean and Flirtology, visit:
www.flirtology.com